MW01128430

SPEAK YOUR WAY TO WEALTH

HOW TO TALK TO YOURSELF, SO YOU CAN SPEAK WITH OTHERS

RICHARD DI BRITANNIA

Originally published in 2021 by Amazon Media EU Sarl. Copyright © 2021 -
Richard Di Britannia.

ISBN: 9798735170358

To Grenville Kleiser, Harry Earnest Hunt and Orison Swett Marden, whose works instilled within me the great virtue of self-improvement.

CONTENTS

FOREWORD

Words are the most powerful drug used by mankind.

RUDYARD KIPLING

As an internationally recognised communication skills coach, voice actor and author, my previous best-selling work '*Speak and Be Heard: 101 Voice Exercises for Voice Actors, Public Speakers and Professionals*' was born from a traumatic incident in early 2012 where, due to a horrific bout of acid reflux, my vocal cords were so damaged I was left mute for months. That book has since been used by a multitude of faces I shall never see whose words will influence innumerable others. It has been added to the libraries of management schools in America, charities in England, and I was even fortunate to receive a letter of gratitude from a schoolmaster using it to teach children in rural India.

This new book *Speak your Way to Wealth – How to Speak to Yourself, so You can Speak with Others* was also influenced from that traumatic incident. For those around me, my being mute may have been a relief to their ears. Yet, what many fail to realise is that when one is unable to speak for a long period of time, the internal dialogue vanishes, the mind begins to fail and the sense of self is lost. Much like the many millions of elderly who succumb to cognitive failure due to a lack of socialisation, so too was I experiencing a similar betrayal of my mind by my ruined vocal cords. As the months passed, I grew increasingly despondent at my situation. My inner voice was failing, my mind was muddied with emotion and I was unable to produce sound to the extent that I would cry should I so much as exhale too harshly. Heaven forbid I should sneeze, as the resulting agony would bring me to my knees in tears. It was at this lowest point that I realised the independence one is granted by having the ability to speak.

Lacking a voice also demonstrated to me the harsh ridicule of the world. As I had no knowledge of sign language or a suitable form of self-expression, when shopping I would carry with me a notepad and pen or a mobile phone app which read my texts aloud to explain to staff my needs. Sadly, many thought I was deaf and I would cast them a wary glance upon hearing the occasional insult towards *"some weirdo with a notepad"* which further reinforced my wish to speak once again. I can only pity those who have suffered a stroke and lost the ability to talk; for being robbed of such a gift is what I consider to be torture. Being able to self-express is liberating. It allows for the communion of countless minds to intermingle and outline what makes us unique. The written word carries little in the way of the subtle nuances of speech and if I had to make a choice, I would far rather lose my ability to write than to speak.

However, like most things of value, this book did not come overly easy to me. There were occasional times when I might have described writing it as *'the hardest thing I have ever done'*. But, upon speaking that thought aloud, I immediately realized its inaccuracy. I have faced far more difficult circumstances - a depressive period lasting seven years, a micro-stroke and a cancer scare were all infinitely more challenging. Yet, in the moment, the thought seemed accurate because my criticality was being usurped by raw emotion. If not for my system of *thought-articulation*, the act of speaking my thoughts aloud, I may never have realised the reality of the situation. The very lesson which this book aims to impart was crucial to its own creation: unarticulated thoughts are often wrong; it is when we speak our own thoughts aloud that we are forced to confront their accuracy or lack-thereof.

As a communication skills coach one of the most beneficial lessons I teach involves building improvisational speaking skills, because the ability to think on one's feet allows my clients to both project and internalise elements of striking self-confidence and generate substantial wealth. When teaching improvisational speaking, it does not mean I instruct clients on how to tell jokes or tall tales - I leave that to the comedians, storytellers and the grandest teacher of all - life. Instead, I teach them my system of *thought-articulation* which allows them to examine and then articulate their thoughts, something which many find fiendishly difficult to do.

Secondly, I wrote this book because I am regularly contacted by clients who have previously attended seminars or worked with other coaches and yet were left empty-handed and lacking proper instruction on how to develop their skills. Expending time and money on tutoring only to essentially be told to 'figure it out' is disheartening to say the least. I too have occasionally fallen victim to gurus with little to offer beyond an over-hyped brand or a reworded truism. A reputable tutor can be discerned by the well-defined, actionable steps they provide to their students. It is my hope that this work is exclusively comprised of such steps.

In my opinion, it is a poor book which offers promises to the reader only to withhold the insightful knowledge befitting of its purchase. To write such a book demonstrates the author sought naught but fame and fortune, rather than to share their wisdom. Therefore, there is no unspoken secret to be found within these pages, there is no mantra to be repeated, nor is there any necessary reading between the lines. The methodology is most simple; regular practice of *thought-articulation* will grant you impromptu eloquence of words and an improved command over the way you communicate with both yourself and others. It is also my hope this work will set a precedent for the quality of education expected from future authors in this industry.

I also write this work not for some profound, spiritual or esoteric reasoning. Instead, I wish to share my knowledge with the world in hope it grants others the abilities I wish had been cultivated in myself decades prior. This book aims not only to grow your articulation skills, but also to instil the great virtue of a self-driven liberal education, not by force, but by suggestion. This book should then dispel a common belief I have heard from many of my students that impromptu and eloquent speech is solely the realm of the elite and the genius. This is untrue. Eloquent improvisation can be learned by anyone with practice. One should never be dismayed by what they see masquerading as impromptu speech in the modern world, for a large amount of supposed unprepared speech on the television, radio or on social media is most certainly anything but. It is often pre-planned, pre-written or even read verbatim and penned by another hand. The reality is that politicians, talking-heads and YouTube celebrities are often merely reading from scripts hidden behind the looking-glass of a teleprompter, reciting pre-rehearsed lines, jokes and retorts, rather than speaking from the heart. Kings, Queens and Presidents have their own speechwriters and it is rare that they speak their own mind. Admittedly, true unbridled *thought-articulation* and impromptu speech is a most challenging art at first, but it is one which can be learned by anyone diligent enough to practice.

This book is therefore for the person who struggles to say what they think. It's for the person who can't seem to find the right words. It's for the person who doesn't know what to say. It will teach them how to articulate thoughts in a manner which will allow for fluent, eloquent and compelling speech.

AUTHOR'S NOTE

I stand here not on the dreams of one, but on the labours of many. We work best when we work together.

STEFAN CROKER

Upon my desk are three volumes of self-instruction manuals for the devotee of public speaking printed in 1908. Only ten years later, readers of those same books would have suffered from or through modern history's worst epidemic – the Spanish Flu of 1918. It is curious then that I should have embarked upon writing this work during the horrific Covid-19 pandemic of 2020. That myself and all those I know would have been like those people of yore, isolated, scared and lonely as we saw those around us suffer from an indiscriminate killer and governments once again fail to act, instead politicising the issue for personal gain. Yet, much as these books upon my desk have survived throughout both periods of turmoil, so too has the human spirit of resilience, camaraderie and generosity.

My editor, Christopher, offered his services to me for this work out of the blue and has, quite frankly, been one of the major driving forces behind ensuring this book was not itself kept isolated in a drawer as an unfinished manuscript. What you read here is a joint effort between both my own mind and his masterful way with words and I feel that if not for his guidance and input this book would have remained merely fragments of my mind occasionally uttered only to my clients. If you should ever need an editor for your own work I wholeheartedly recommend *Christopher Lee Winn*. You can contact him at: ChristopherLeeWinn.com

INTRODUCTION

> *You can speak well if your tongue can deliver the message of your heart.*
>
> JOHN FORD

This book can be summarised in three words: *speak to yourself.* If you are a glutton for information, it can be expounded into five: *articulate your thoughts precisely, aloud.* The problem is that without knowing how, those simple instructions can be fiendishly difficult.

Cast your mind back to a moment when you heard someone fail to articulate themselves well. We have all seen these moments and they are often memorable, if not for the right reasons. How regularly does a speaker launch into telling a story which lacks an impressionable ending? How about those who merely repeat a number of buzzwords, soundbites or talking points which they clearly failed to understand? What of those who stare open-mouthed into the camera making a series of noises as they try to grasp their thoughts after a sudden turn in an interview? In almost all instances, it would have been better if they had said nothing at all – their silence could not have been misquoted.

When you hear people fail to articulate their thoughts and instead bumble along without understanding what they say, do you hold them in high regard? Do you praise their blustering? Perhaps there are moments when you empathise with them, because at some point we have all done the same. Yet, ask yourself do you wish to emulate them?

The people who once criticised your speech as a child usually only did so because they were paid enough to care – this does not continue in the adult world. As an adult what you say must become valuable, because if not you will make little impact in the world and be relegated to the ranks of the underpaid, or worse yet, the forgotten.

It can be incredibly embarrassing, frustrating and detrimental to our self-confidence when we sabotage our standing with unprepared words. Despite initially launching into discussion with confidence and zeal, it is only when we open our mouths and find the lacklustre words at our disposal betray our initial exuberance. Realising we have little of merit to say, our attempts to formulate an opinion without preparation often leave us attempting to explain our thoughts to ourselves, rather than to our listeners. Circumlocution begins, the heart races and we faulter as growing anxiety demands we retreat into awkward silence.

That then is the crux of the matter – the articulate speaker understands what they think at a subconscious level allowing them to communicate their thoughts effortlessly. *They do not speak to explain their thoughts to themselves any further, instead they speak to teach their preconsidered thoughts to others.* By the effort of intellectual osmosis, they have improved their level of thinking to being able to clearly articulate how they feel without falling into the trap of paying attention to their thoughts, rules of style or methods of delivery.

Read the points below and then *speaking your thoughts aloud*, question yourself:

- What do you lack in abilities to achieve success?

- What have you not accomplished?

- How can you better manage your life?

- How can you best improve your abilities?

- What daily activities need the largest improvement?

- Are you fitting yourself for a larger purpose?

- Who can you learn from in person?

- Is hesitation or a weakness holding you back?

- Do you have a goal in mind and are you taking daily steps to work towards it?

- How many of these problems can be helped with better thought-articulation skills?

Introspection is a most difficult process when one is unable to articulate their feelings. Yet, by answering these questions it shall demonstrate to you the importance of improving your ability to communicate well to both yourself and others will improve your life as a whole. The answers you struggle with will also diagnose any self-imposed limitations which are crippling you in your capabilities and potential.

However, if after answering these questions you still feel as if you lack the courage to speak before others or think for yourself, take solace in the fact that throughout history you can find records of hundreds of once meek men and women who despite in their youth hiding from public view later gained the confidence, charisma and capabilities to stand tall and speak their mind before their peers. Across all cultures, creeds and communities there are countless celebrities, scientists, actors, musicians, writers, teachers, businessmen and similarly great talents who once struggled to communicate, yet through earnest effort eventually empowered their mind and voiced their thoughts.

If you can articulate your thoughts without being crippled by self-introspection, stammering from thought-paralysis or left open-mouthed by lack of knowledge you will become a force to be reckoned with. Few hold confidence in their thoughts to the degree that they may talk about them without restraint. Yet, it is this level of expertise which causes rooms to fall silent at the marvelling of some majestic maestro of words who communicates so effortlessly that their wisdom seems to be pulled from the air itself. In reality, the speaker is no genius, instead they understand their thoughts to the degree that they can articulate them in a myriad of ways without hesitation; for at a subconscious level the rapidity of their mind will cast away improper prose, rhyme and reason at ease.

To reach this level of expertise requires constant daily study of your thoughts, but there is an often repeated quote which claims *'most people would rather die than think'*. Carl Jung similarly wrote *'thinking is difficult, that's why most people judge',* but I don't believe these views to be absolutes. I'm not cynical enough. However, I have found that for some, thinking and thought-articulation is incredibly difficult – instead, people plead for someone else to translate their emotions into the spoken word. Further still, many seem to be scared of speaking their mind. This is not because they harbour some kind of vile viewpoint, but because they are fearful of being misunderstood. Deep down, they do not truly understand their own thoughts. In comparison, being able to speak your mind in eloquent and clear terms shows you have a clear understanding of your own ideas. When you speak with such power, you will communicate with confidence and a depth of thought which has the potential to place you in positions of authority, prestige and influence.

The ability to articulate your thoughts will aid you in becoming a master of charming debates and a persuasive winner of hearts and minds. Yet, these debates will not be argumentative feuds which serve only to drive a wedge between others. They will be deliberations in which you empower both yourself and those around you with the outlining of your ideals, philosophies and the shining of your brilliant choice of words. Of course, many will agree with you, others will dispute you, but with an articulate mind you will have the strength to defend yourself with your words to disarm those who seek to demean you.

Moreover, with improved communication skills comes clarity of thought and wisdom. With this you will see through the constant bombardment of obscuring and twisted rhetoric which usurps rationality. You will question if your snap judgement is reflective of your current beliefs or merely a remnant of a base instinct or indoctrinated mantra. You will also understand where your own weaknesses lie, for no-one knows your mind better than yourself. Few are able to explain who they really are and what they truly think, but through thought-articulation you will gain insight to *know thyself*.

Being able to articulate your thoughts clearly will also have the surprising effect of potentially changing your mind. Many a time I have articulated a thought aloud, only to recant my initial reactive emotions. Similarly, I have known clients who were once dogmatic and binary in their judgements due to a lack of introspection to justify their beliefs. Yet, after reading widely, listening to others and attempting to orate their principles, it led to the realisation that their thoughts were merely the recitation of words or concepts enforced upon them during early development, or pressures from their environment, rather than their own true feelings. Introspective-articulation and the questioning if their pre-existed thoughts reflected their current ideals lead to a revaluation of their identity. This introspection ultimately allowed for them to abandon antiquated ideologies and replace such relicts with beliefs formed by their own thinking. Such a flourishing is liberating to the soul and allows for enormous spiritual growth.

The improvement of being able to articulate your thoughts correspondingly leads to an increase in emotional intelligence. We all know of someone who has a short temper, who kicks and screams at barricades and shouts at long-suffering workers for no reason. Few of us ever wish to be that person. Yet, the ability to manage one's emotions by translating once ephemeral feelings into comprehendible language almost always reduces our levels of aggression. You need only look to the prisons to see leagues of men and women who, lacking the ability to comprehend their passions, have let emotions, violence and illogical thoughts ruin their lives. An individual with low emotional intelligence and poor thought-articulation may not be able to differentiate between *anger* and *frustration* – leading to them latching onto the most base feelings and so cruelty becomes their universal solution.

Through thought-articulation you are also less likely to be animalistically reactive to negative experiences and instead take upon a more elegant form which is reflective and considerate of consequences if you can articulate your true emotions. Further still, increased emotional intelligence allows for you to better empathise with the needs of others, resulting in greater social awareness of how your words and actions impact the world around you. This ability to prevent inter-personal conflict allows for a greater social cohesion which cannot be underestimated. From this, mindfulness usually follows, granting the ability to cast aside negative thoughts and focus on the positive. Despite what the stoic philosophers may say, emotion almost always usurps rationality, but this complex should not run our lives for we are the *Invictus*; the masters of our fate and the captains of our soul.

What then of the wider impact? Improving how you articulate your thoughts can also help with identifying how others think. In business, if one party primarily talks in mechanical metaphors by saying 'the product will *skyrocket*' whilst another talks in naturalistic terms by saying 'the product will *grow*', the message conveyed can be similar yet misunderstood. The first speaker may be a logical-minded type who believes rapid sales are soon to follow, whereas the other speaker may be a more emotional individual who is bearish on sales. Not examining these differences can be catastrophic to business and personal relations.

Improving your thought-articulation further allows for a directness of speech. Much like it would be difficult to reach a destination if you were to set sail at sea without a compass, so too it is difficult to speak your thoughts without a topic in mind. A demonstration of this is being asked to 'say something'; wherein the speaker often stumbles and repeats something trite they have heard, or asks 'what do you want me to say' rather than engage in immediate critical thought-articulation. When no narrative has been set, thoughts will be sparse and speech will be mere sound. It is only the pre-rehearsal of thoughts which allow for a sudden springing into action.

Enhanced thought-articulation skills will later allow for one to summarise information into succinct chunks which are easily understood and explained. Compare this to the long-winded stories you may be familiar with where a speaker doubles back to explain their thoughts to themselves multiple times in a conversation rather than continuing forward. Their mind now knotted into loops is twisted into an irregular shape attempting to force square words into round holes.

What then of further influence? The reality is people tend to agree with those who are able to articulate their thoughts in nimble ways – regardless of those words being true or false. Lucidity of speech will portray you as a precise and ordered thinker and motivate others to seek out your advice. Being sought after for your clarity of expression is a prestigious position and such standing will foster respect for your abilities and contributions – alongside increased wealth. As a lucid communicator, audiences will give you time to speak rather than interrupt your points with their own. Nothing is more enjoyable to a speaker than realising you are valued by others for your mere thoughts and your words can increase the weight of your wallet.

Confidence in your other abilities will also grow with improved thought-articulation. Practice of self-introspection will naturally lead to greater self-mastery. Gracefully stating '*I don't know enough to form an opinion*' is far more eloquent than spouting an uninformed comment. With practice, you will ultimately no longer be one of those awkward people who say something foolish to fill necessary silence.

Finally, with the ability to clearly and confidently articulate your thoughts, you will learn the most important skill of all – how to listen. The words *listen* and *silent* are made of the same letters. One should not only talk, but also sit quietly at the feet of giants to learn but also listen intently to those of lesser abilities to understand and empathise. The human body has two ears and a single mouth and should be used in such ratio – many an earning has been made through silent observation alone.

CHAPTER 1

ALL EYES ON YOU

The pen has discovered many a genius, but the process is slower and less effective than the singular great occasion which discovers the humble orator.

ORISON SWETT MARDEN

It's lonely here being the centre of attention. Stood before hundreds of eyes and ears focused intently on your every word - on this stage you may have no friends. Your heart is racing, you feel as if you want to flee, but your time is not yet finished. The show must go on. You're uncomfortable and why wouldn't you be, wrapped in twenty foot of coarse white wool, a burdensome garment restricting your movement, weighing you down and leaving you covered in sweat. Your passion is evident but, every movement you make is carefully practiced to prevent the folds of this attire slipping from your shoulders. As you talk, each pre-planned and delicate gesture beckons only to one person at a time. Your eyes scan the audience and see faces smile, grimace

1

and stare. Reminiscent of an elegant statue, you plead your case before a capricious audience of your peers which swings from silent rapture to cacophonous hatred.

Why are you here? A simple reason. Your precious patch of land is to be torn asunder under the marching boots of foreign powers and it is your duty to plead for aid before your home and livelihood is left pillaged and decimated. From childhood you have been trained in the art of coining rhetoric, pondering philosophy and instilling to others the importance of earnest debate. Your speech is liable to last for two hours or more and you are unlikely to have notes to hand. This is the life of an ancient Roman citizen and as one of these people, it is your responsibility to stand tall, speak up and state your case.

Yet you? You are a modern-day citizen. You probably have no formal speech training; you are unprepared, you're scared, but you have to give that speech. It's only a small one. It's only to a few people. But why are you trembling? Why can't you think straight? You know what you want to say, but why can't you say it? If you can't articulate your thoughts, you can't speak well. If you can't speak well, you can't express yourself to others. If you can't express yourself to others, you can't advance and if you can't advance, someone else will.

Sadly, this is the case for many, because most are no longer confident enough to speak for themselves. No longer are people trained in the art of debate, instead lawyers are more than happy to speak on their behalf for an exorbitant fee.

In school, children are beaten with the proverbial stick of being *'seen, but not heard'*. Such schooling is more likely to chastise them for a mistake rather than advise on how to grow their confidence.

Election polls show millions no longer recognise malicious rhetoric; if they did, they would not vote against their interests for those who rob them of their rights and empty their wallets.

Right-wing talking heads demonise anyone unlike themselves yet are seen as bastions of 'truth'. Far-left ideals spurred-on by fallacious memes have replaced critical thought, economic reason and their famine-causing legacies are once again being considered as an alternative to Capitalism.

Further still, in government we hear communication in circumlocution, spin doctors advising our elected officials to avoid scrutiny by obfuscation and a growing demonisation of science and logic. The highest levels of office bumble and spew nonsense before our eyes – yet people accept it, because many dare not speak up and others merely accept the lies to be true.

However, there are some who have grown tired of the tricks, the fabrications and the pretentiousness given by these elites and talking heads whose connection to the people extends only to the ground upon which they walk. There are some who wish to see through the veil of rhetoric. There are some who wish to speak their mind. There are some who wish to empower themselves with linguistic force. These are the people like yourself who wish to speak for themselves rather than repeat talking points; who wish to control their mind rather than let it be controlled by advertisers; who demand to respond rather than react. Like you, these are the people who wish to empower their children to no longer sit in silence; who wish to use the right of free speech to fight with their words, not their fists; who wish to speak and be heard. It is my aim that by following the exercises detailed in this book, yourself and others like you will one day be able to exclaim *'what I say, I have said myself!'*

Yet, there is nothing more paralysing than being unable to articulate the thoughts in your mind. It's torturous. It's agonising. In that moment of verbal breakdown, the mind runs wild with thoughts immaterial, cloudy and undefined. In desperation for the right words the eyes search, the hands grasp and the tongue errs in apology. When a word is finally found it is rarely ideal and another takes its place. The speaker halts, stalls and stumbles. The following phrases are stifled, others are kept on the tip of the tongue unuttered. The paralysis continues, the heart races, the breathing worsens. This is the moment when one knows what to say, but doesn't know how to say it and all the eyes watching know it too.

Yet if you can speak, if you can articulate your thoughts, if you can impress upon other people of your ideas, give them values which change the way they act and inspire others - you will be among the most influential people in the world.

Knowing this, does some lingering fear still resonate with you? Amongst almost all my clients I have found they agree. They feel their use of words is either lacking, verbose or not reflective of how they think. Others feel crippled by the stares from their audiences. Some find themselves speaking in circles; starting one phrase and then ending on an unrelated other. Unable to say what they feel this fear diminishes them, punishes them and denigrates their true abilities. They feel as if they are a fool, an idiot or an imposter. I am regularly beholden to nod along to these students, professionals and occasional multi-millionaire CEO's whose attempts to express even simple thoughts results in nonsensical statements like; '...so, urr, yea, you know what I mean, like?' followed by an awkward shrug and admission of defeat that *no*, we don't '*know what you mean, like*'.

Is this not a shame? It is painful to see these intelligent and passionate people skirmish against their own minds in effort to articulate their thoughts. Viewers to this spectacle can clearly see the inward battle being waged against the realm of non-existent emotional thought and that of materialised speech. But what is to be done? How can one overcome this paralysis? How does one find the right words?

It is through long and determined meditation that I have concluded there is no better exercise than the practice of what I coin *thought-articulation*; the act of articulating your thoughts with intense effort - on a random topic - without preparation - for a short amount of time. With practice, *thought-articulation* can be adopted for *extemporaneous speech*; the art of speaking impromptu and reciting malleable pre-formed thoughts at whim. Ironically, speaking your thoughts aloud sounds quite simple, but it can be fiendishly difficult. More than one of my students has referred to the practice of *thought-articulation* as '*two minutes from Hell*' on their maiden attempt.

Alas! Do not be afraid, this is no Satanic ritual. Nor do you need to practice in public; no exercise is more perilous than to stand before an audience and attempt to express your thoughts concisely without pre-prepared support. Nothing else demonstrates an apparent weakness of mind, poverty of imagination and limitation of vocabulary than to falter when speaking - even if the said faults are not reflective of your abilities.

Thankfully, the practice detailed in this book does not demand you assemble an audience and talk at length on some complex topic. Nor does it demand you give a studious lecture free from faults on some abstract theorem. Instead it suggests you choose one of the many common subjects provided or a theme you are well versed with and by following the framework outlined throughout this book adapt it to best suit your needs.

Of course, thought-articulation is still challenging. It can often be punishing too, because it outlines exactly where our weaknesses lie. Yet, with competence comes confidence and hundreds of students have shown me that regular practice of this short exercise will aid in enormously increasing both your verbal fluency and quickness of mind.

Here then I give you my word that when you have acted upon the advice given in this book, changed the way you think and invested the time to speak on all the provided topics in your private practice, you will notice a significant change in the quality of your life and the way others respond to your words.

First and foremost, through vocalised introspection your thoughts will become deeper, more refined and increasingly individualistic. You will no longer be at the whim of reactionary thought lacking criticality, swayed by mob mentality; instead you will furnish them with deep introspection which will carry you up the ladder of progress in business and your personal life. With a depth of thought brought about by orated internal dialogue, your mind will be forced into conceiving new ideas and casting aside those which were once seen as unshakable mental bastions. The humourist Josh Billings (1847) once wrote '*...it ain't so much the things that people don't know that makes trouble in this world, as it is the things that people know that ain't so*' – he was right. For if you cannot articulate a position to the point that you could convince someone-else of it, then you likely do not understand it well enough to strongly counter objections against it.

Further still, by speaking on the various topics provided, your words will become more elegant, more well-chosen and easier to understand. Talking in public, be it to a lone listener or a crowd of a hundred will one-day become a joy for both you and your audience, rather than a bore for them and a fear for you. With clarity of thought comes eloquent delivery. The clear thinker who is also an eloquent communicator inevitably becomes a leader. Everyone is, in their fashion, seeking a comprehendible Truth - a solid rock amidst sinking sand. A storyteller about the campfire. A guiding light amidst a storming tempest. Those cultivated people who offer such a gift to others are the wheel on which the human world turns, whether they be in the boardroom or across the dinner table.

What you do with this influence will be your life's legacy. If you still feel the exertion demanded is too strenuous, know that the practice of thought-articulation is nothing in comparison to the many hundreds, if not thousands of hours required by the musician to play a handful of notes. At your command you already have before you tens of thousands of words. Through regular practice, they can grant you the power to demand whatever you desire.

IT ISN'T CRAZY TO TALK TO YOURSELF

What we say is important for in most cases the mouth speaks what the heart is full of.

JIM BEGGS

When I walk around the park near my home, people must think I am quite mad, because I talk to myself.

I talk to myself concerning all topics. I observe the trees and describe them aloud. I notice an interesting pattern and give a private lecture on its structure. I attempt to define a random thought which passes through my mind. All this must be quite concerning to those around me and sometimes little of it is articulate. Yet, if I were to name one habit which develops the mind so fully aside the acts of writing and reading, it would be to cast aside all shame and talk to yourself whenever you can.

Reading this you may already disagree with me. You wouldn't be the first to do so. There seems to be some overarching repugnance in being told to talk to ourselves. As a child, you may have been told not to talk to yourself; it's not something adults do. Perhaps instead you may have been told those who talk to themselves are insane or suffering from a mental illness, but this is not always the case. You may perhaps be scared that someone should walk into a room whilst you are mid-oration. Yet, I strongly press you to disregard the idea that talking to yourself is a detrimental act, because teaching this concept to hundreds of clients across all ages and social standing has found it to be transformative.

Of course, you should not talk in public in attempt to enlighten others on subjects you do not truly understand – that is folly. Instead, it is the free and creative self-talk which is most beneficial in developing your communication skills.

Why then does speaking aloud work better than merely thinking? Surely if you can hear a voice inside our head when we think, that would suffice? Although this argument is logical, it breaks down in reality. When thinking, thought arrives in a convoluted, abstract and often indefinable manner like wisps of fog carried along by the winds. The mind can also run at a pace far greater than speech, like the darting of a passing insect compared to our slow eyes. Further still, due to *mental blind spots* the missing of obvious mistakes occurs, because the brain is more likely to rapidly jump from one topic to the next without scrutiny, rather than engage in critical thought when we are thinking in emotional states.

What more, lacking a structure our thoughts are further interrupted, side-tracked and derailed by fleeting impulses. Being unspoken our numerous partialised emotions remain in a perpetual state of immaterial and unactionable feelings. In comparison, coherent speech requires words to follow strict grammatical rules with little deviation acceptable at a comparatively slow pace. Much like a painter is first required to separate each individual colour upon their palette rather than blending them all into one oil tube; if you wish to articulate your feelings, your thoughts are required to be transformed into coherent sentences abiding by grammatical rules containing nouns, verbs, adjectives and so-forth.

By talking to yourself, it forces your mind to draw upon the many hues of your lexicon. Lexicographical limitations often identify weaknesses, for instance, an overreliance of filler words such as *'umm', 'err'* or *'like'*. It can also show if we are verbose with our words meaning we never really get to the point, or it can simply allude how we lack the knowledge necessary to expand our thoughts.

Given this, I have found *it is the inability to articulate these feelings which causes many to feel despondent, rather than any lack of intelligence.* When tasking students to practice thought-articulation the first thing to break down is usually not the recollection of knowledge, but the formation of grammatical structure, because the mind is so taxed in articulating emotional concepts that it cannot function. When this occurs, the student will either admit defeat entirely, retreat back to the beginning of the thought, or attempt to soldier on forward and push past the mental blockade. Students who refuse to retreat and restate their case are those who meet with the most rapid success. Refusing to loop backwards, the student soon gains the ability to speak in a coherent manner, whereas the student who retreats quickly becomes locked into taxing circumlocution.

Is it not strange how frequently we can be lost in silent thought, struggling to answer a problem or articulate a proposal and yet when we attempt to explain this problem to a friend or colleague fresh ideas bubble up from the subconscious and provide us with the answers we seek? It is not the questioning from our friends which provides the answer (for they have not studied the same subject), nor is it their agreement or disagreement with our proposals, but the verbalised articulation of the once abstract emotional thought into well-defined words which aid us in solving the problem at hand. In reality, we already had the knowledge we sought – it simply needed to be said aloud.

Perhaps you may recollect a time when you were struggling immensely with formulating an answer to a question. Left in the despair of mental bankruptcy you chose to abandon the affair for a length of time, only for the answer to suddenly appear in the mind. The knowledge therefore already existed, it was merely the articulation of thoughts which were at fault. It is in my experience that once this mote of inspiration occurs people usually begin to articulate their thoughts aloud in effort to solidify the conclusion into tangible words. Odd then that this comes naturally and yet, people are often too shy to practice it at will.

Why then do we do not articulate our thoughts more often? Probably because as mentioned earlier, if you speak to yourself, you're going to be worried about being perceived as 'crazy' to others, but it's not crazy at all. In fact, I've yet to meet a single person who didn't talk to themselves at least once or twice a day.

Usually, this self-talk occurs when they were trying to articulate an emotional sensation and one of the hardest emotional sensations to articulate is that of a 'gut feeling'. In this context, a gut feeling is separate from intuition. It would be best defined as an immediate, subconscious identification of a threat or opportunity presented in an emotional manner. For example, if one sees an individual approaching them and experiences a gut feeling stating *'this person is a threat'*, the subconscious will fill the mind with the desire to avoid the individual to prevent potential confrontation. In identifying the formation of this desire, the subconscious has likely recognised something threatening about the individual's body language or appearance which has resonated with a traumatic past experience or perceived knowledge. However, if one were to attempt to articulate the said gut feeling, they would often struggle to explain exactly why they had such a reaction. Plausible reasons may be the individual's clothing, mannerisms or body language not aligning with the expected norms, but the reality is that the subconscious merely provided an abstract *emotional* warning, rather than a specifically defined and articulated linguistic thought. Articulating the emotional warning would lead to deep introspection into one's past experiences, which can be transformative.

Interestingly, fear of self-talk rarely occurs in children who are especially creative problem solvers. For a large portion of their early development, children will talk to themselves whilst attempting to articulate their imaginations, emotions and so forth. It is only until the 'responsible' adult tells them not to speak to themselves that this practice ends, causing the child to increasingly stumble with articulating their thoughts. Similarly, it is often when a child is told to think in silence that the wonders of imagination begin to vanish. In my view, this demand is especially damaging to the child, because it stifles their ability to articulate their thoughts, ideas and solve problems.

Further still the practice of articulating thoughts aloud allows for the development of several areas of the brain responsible for speech development, namely the *Broca's area* and *Wernicke's area*. Through the development of these areas, translation of ephemeral thought into vocalised speech becomes easier. With regular practice, one will quickly find how a rapid transformation of thought into spoken word allows for a liberating sense of self expression. Now able to explain exactly how they feel; the speaker can grant linguistic form upon feelings once mired by untranslatable emotions and abstract imagery.

What are the other benefits of talking to yourself? First and foremost, it will allow for a greater comprehension of your thoughts, which, when given form into defined terms can be acted upon promptly. Second, it will grant you the ability to improve upon your word recollection skills, gifting you a lucidity of words and phrases at your disposal. Third, by the effort of articulating abstract thought into conceptualised form it will prepare you for those inopportune moments when one is met with a complex question from a concerned party which leaves little time for consideration. A hasty recollection of pre-established ideas which have already been uttered in previous practice will serve as valuable ammunition against onslaught.

However, before you begin it is necessary to outline the common mistakes which new practitioners of thought-articulation make.

A common pitfall many of my clients initially experience is regurgitating all information they can recollect into one stream of thought devoid of pauses. This should be avoided, especially when speaking during a two-minute timeslot, because such practice ultimately leads to incoherence and a

SPEAK YOUR WAY TO WEALTH

lack of oxygen. It isn't possible to breathe and talk at the same time. The voice works on air, but the lungs and brain need it more! You should therefore aim to initially identify the topic at hand, quickly collect your thoughts, compose an opening sentence and then launch yourself full-heartedly into discussion ensuring to take regular pauses. Circumlocution is inevitable during early practice, but this should not be seen as a detriment because with each attempt improvement will follow.

Students also often tell me they can write far better than they can speak which demoralises them. I understand why, because I feel the same. Yet, the reality is that written words are pre-planned and take often a hundred times longer to write than one takes to speak. Thought is reined in by the use of the pen, because the pen cannot move as rapidly as the mind. Therefore, you should not hold your everyday speech to the same standard as your written work. To do so is to engage in a false economy; the mere act of writing is far slower than even the most pondersome of talker.

I hope by now, I will therefore have convinced you that the first requisite for eloquent speaking is the clothing of words in *previously conceived and privately orated* thoughts. Imagine then, how marvellous it would be if you had the ability to tailor these words and convince your listener of the effortlessness of what appears to be a mere off-the-cuff speech, whilst simultaneously hiding your efforts in practice; granting you the appearance as a master of the impromptu spoken word. Of course, some will struggle more than others. The student who has dedicated their life to the study of the classics will have an advantage over the desultory reader of the newspaper, because thought-matter is made up of what is added to the mind. However, the majesty of the mind allows for anyone, of any standing in society, to advance through its ranks by earnest practice and unwavering faith.

If you fill your mind with great ideas and articulate your resounding thoughts aloud, you will grant yourself an ability to speak with skill which will far surpass that which you have now.

CONFLICT BEGINS WHEN COMMUNICATION CEASES

A mind at peace does not engender wars.

SOPHOCLES

Second only to brandishing a rock or stick, communication by voice is our earliest ancestor. Be it grunts, clicks, guttural sounds or song, verbal communication has been found amongst every culture, every religion and every society in the world. It is inescapable. It is influential. It is powerful. Thankfully, most people have dropped the rock and stick and instead use their voice to convey their thoughts.

The phonetic combination of vowels and consonants in their myriad of ways producing vibrations traveling from the throat through the air and striking a minute timpani-esque drum, which through the near-magical majesty of the brain translates these waves of sound into words cannot be overappreciated.

Words have the power to incite, words have the power to sooth and words have the power to be appropriate or inappropriate. Words can be used to wage war or plead for peace. Words are the backbone of our society; without them there would be no thought, no culture, no progress.

Van-Gogh is pleasing to the eye, but the spoken word of Shakespeare is fathomless and in the right hands, a microphone can be more powerful than a gun.

But what happens when you cannot express these thoughts? What happens when you cannot explain these concepts? What happens when you just can't find the words? Conflict. Conflict in a myriad of ways. Conflict with the self. Conflict with others. Conflict with the world. Conflict only begins when communication ceases. Consider the millions of lives lost at the hands of a weapon for the sake of a conversation. Consider the families torn apart and children oppressed for the sake of poorly worded political messages. Consider the jobs lost and hungry mouths gone unfed for the sake of a misspoken phrase in the workplace. Consider also the conflict inside your mind when you simply cannot find the words to express how you feel.

Similarly, why is it when challenged to prepare a speech, most protest in silence? Is this not conflict? The reality is they dare not speak up in protest for life has taught them not to. After the initial anxiety has passed and a stiff drink has been poured, they rest their palm against their head, ruffle their hair and then put pen to paper, only to vomit a stream of consciousness and a rambling of ideas onto the page. When called to speak the final result is usually lacking style, order and impact.

Worse yet, if challenged to speak on the spot, many break out into a cold sweat. They bluster, stutter and splinter their words as their minds turn inwards. Their anxiety flairs, their heart races, their voices break and their eyes show they are screaming internally whilst they commit kamikaze by words. Their speech is a chore to listen to or a disastrous mess which serves only to confuse the listener and diminish the hidden abilities of the speaker. But this need not be so.

Perhaps the old hackneyed *Seinfeld* quote that *"fear of death outranks fear of public speaking"* comes to mind. Admittedly, despite my years of practice, there are still moments during informal round-table events when myself and many others like me feel our hearts begin to race knowing that we are expected to speak next. There is much debate between sociologists and biologists if this fear is either a learned or inherited trait, but I have found learning of its origins does little to prevent such worries. Rather, it is better to note how even the oratorical giants of antiquity likely wrote how 'taking the stage felt as if Old Man Winter had plunged his icy fingers into their heart seconds before mounting those three accursed steps'.

You may never completely remove the fear of speaking unprepared or find the perfect word every time, but through practice you can give yourself a stable footing to stand upon and talk true. Whereas once you may have been terrified of falling afoul of struggling with a word 'on the tip of your tongue', this hindrance will be replaced with improved memory and fluency over a few short weeks. Further still, being able to articulate your thoughts makes you a near-unstoppable force in the realm of public debate, because no-matter what question is thrown at you, you will always be able to answer it succinctly. You may even realise your belief was wrong and then articulate your immediate change of opinion, placing you in high esteem with your opponents.

Through the practicing of thought-articulation, I have found in hundreds of instances that it can transform once timid and shy near-stutterers into confident and well-spoken articulators, each brimming with mental quickness, resourcefulness and charisma. Now able to articulate their thoughts clearly, they gain a both a crystal-clear vision for their ideals and a mental suit of armour alongside their newfound self-expression which protects them from concern. When practiced over a year or more, the repeated struggle instils within the speaker a level of confidence, coherence and conciseness of thought once unimagined that begins to permeate all areas of life, bestowing upon the speaker a masterful ability to weave long forgotten memories into alluring prose and a maestro-like capability to apparently compose sage aphorisms drawn from naught but the aether.

To think and speak free and true of your own accord is to live your life liberated, to show to others who you are, to refuse to be bound by the shackles of silent obedience to the words of others. As the neurologist, psychiatrist, philosopher, author and Holocaust survivor *Viktor Frankl* (1095 – 2007) wrote in *Man's Search for Meaning* (1946), one can be stripped of all worldly possessions, dignity and betrayed by those around him, yet no force on Earth can cause one with a strong mind to accept thoughts or say things they do not believe in.

If you can be diplomatic with your words, state your case and engage in dialogue, you will quickly find that all other forms of conflict will disappear. As long as you are talking, you're not truly fighting.

TALK LIKE AN IMMORTAL

Let thy speech be better than silence, or be silent.

DIONYSIUS OF HALICARNASSUS

Conversation with an immortal being would be agonising, because they probably wouldn't reply in your lifetime.

Immortality would be either a paradise like gift or an eternity of endless suffering. Disease and disaster would be of little consequence; it would be boredom which bred discontent. Assuming their memories didn't degrade over time, to stave off the monotony an immortal could embark upon projects which would last longer than the sum of thousands of human lifespans. An immortal could practice painting in a single medium continually for a hundred decades before being satisfied. An immortal-led theatrical play could last for a millennium uninterrupted and why not? It would stave off waiting for the heat death of the universe. Infinite life would bring about changes to our minds beyond the comprehension of even our most astute scholars and philosophers – what would minds be like which had seen stars born and die?

For the immortal, their communication skills would change into something quite alien to what we experience in our mere mortal lives. Conversation with one would be the duty of generations, fathers passing down the topic to their daughters, only for them to pass that same topic onto their sons, all at the behest of the immortal's wish for "time to think". Endless time.

Whereas we take a microsecond to pause and find the 'right word', an immortal would have grown tired of being misunderstood over the millennia and instead would probably ponder for decades upon end in effort to articulate their thoughts to encapsulate the perfect, unimpeachable response.

With unlimited time at their disposal, their lexicons would be beyond the scope of our greatest poets and polyglots. They could dip in between languages dead and alive to find words, phrases and expressions which best reflected their emotional state. Their choice of words and extremes of emotion perfected over aeons would be more polished than any of the works ever produced by mankind allowing them to write the wisest books, sing siren-like songs and compose the most moving music. With this knowledge they could answer any question; assuming you lived long enough to hear it.

Further still, a talk between *two* immortals could outlive an entire planet - each sat in silence as the world crumbled to ruin around them as they mused. A dying planet would be of no matter. They could survive floating in the void of space to think a little longer, or build a craft to travel elsewhere if they thought the response was going to arrive in a few years' time.

Immortals would probably also have little in the way of small-talk. What would be the point? If you were to ask them if anything had happened 'recently' they may have a skewed meaning of the concept. Yesterday? In the last decade? The last million years? Intellectual beings are creative and these immortal beings would have far more important things to do than gossip. A little nudge here, a little push there and suddenly they are the dictator or liberator of an entire galaxy. They could act as empire builders or great destroyers. They could gamify the event, seeing who could rise to prominence the fastest or pull the most subtle of strings with the direst of consequences. Throughout all this fun, why indulge in small-talk? Our mortal conversations, worries and joys concerning the daily trivialities of life would be banal in comparison to their grand schemes. Instead, their conversations would probably exist only to further the abilities of their race, rather than to talk about the weather.

Of course, we are not immortal and sadly I doubt any of us will live to experience such an event in our lifespans. But let's be honest; a majority of daily conversation is banal, unproductive and even potentially damaging to your abilities to communicate. Therefore, you should learn how speak like an immortal and sometimes choose to forgo mindless chatter.

To some, this may be a radical proposal. There can be joy to be found in gossip and everyday talk. Yet, much like eating unhealthy food every day would destroy the body, everything must be done in moderation. In my research for this book, I have found regular unproductive talk is one of the singular most detrimental activities to both thought and speech.

Let me tell you why.

SMALL TALK, SMALL IDEAS

Raise your words, not your voice.

RUMI

"If you's time to think lad, then you's time to drink, so shut it, get a pint down ye and don't make waves. Understand?"

"Don't make waves". Those were the words etched into the minds of the members of a narrowboating community I lived with during my teenage years.

Intending to live a quiet life free from the trifles of landlocked labour, this rag-tag group of ex-hippies, rockers and former Masons expressed only a desire to accept things as they were, to never press for change nor speak up. Discussion was relegated to the weather, to football or to complaints about the 'state' of England. At an average age of Retired, their incentive to do new things or think new thoughts was largely confined to sailing

England's canals in search of the next pub, next pint or most rare of all, next sun spot.

Yet, on occasion when they returned from an excursion they would learn that yet another sailor had slipped from the jetty, hit their head on the way down and drowned - probably due to management reducing the walk-space by another six inches leaving nothing but a plank or two to walk atop. Alas, death was hardly worth speaking up about, was it? That might cause trouble! That might cause questions to be asked, people to be held responsible, someone to get upset or heaven forbid – someone to have a deep conversation. They couldn't have that. No-no, life was to stay exactly as it was. Everyone was to stay quiet and no-one was to make waves either when sailing or speaking. After all, a shrug of the shoulder and tug upon the bottle would sooth all woes, because *"...thinking won't do you any good lad, but a bottle of this will."*

It is clear to me now that their quasi-Daoism or faux-Zen had little to do with actually accepting reality and being freed of resentment. It was instead apathy. Denying one's own ability to better their world is an illusion just as grandiose as the unobtainable wrought by the Utopian, who thinks they would have all the answers if only they had total power.

However, not everyone who fails to think and speak up is engaging in excuse-making or apathy. Working with brave, bold and even boisterous clients has shown me that for some, failing to think and engage in deep conversation is the result of years of repeated moments of mindless chatter which has, like a perished limb, undermined their communication skills and weakened that mental muscle.

Surveying nearly two-hundred of my clients to observe their daily conversation between friends, colleagues and family showed startling results. More than 70% stated that before their second lesson with me, their daily conversation consisted of primarily unthinking acceptances such as *"yeah, I suppose..."*, aimless chatter to fill silence, such as; *"what did you think of the game last night?"* or un-contesting deferrals such as; *"I dunno, what do you think?"*. In comparison to what would have been hoped for, little in the way of well-articulated speech was being expressed on a daily basis. Small talk it seemed, had grown quite large.

In this study I also found more than 40% expressed they engaged in less than one deep conversation or moment of introspective thought a month – potentially explaining the communication issues faced amongst this minority.

The participants were also asked to rate their ability to articulate their thoughts to themselves in either writing or self-talk. In this, once again more than 70% stated they felt as if they were struggling to express their ideas in an effective manner, with the most common complaint being an inability to define the crux of their emotional state or outline what they were thinking in solid terms. Artists are well versed with a similar issue, the image they see in their mind is rarely the image which is produced on canvas.

However, with every study there are outliers. In rare occasions a client did engage in some form of deep conversation or thought on a daily basis. Cross-referencing these results to my coaching notes I found these clients were without exception the exemplary communicators who sought polish for their enunciation, rather than improvement in their communication skills. Further investigating these outliers showed these individuals were placed in positions which were liable to stimulate a need for regular thought-articulation; many worked in highly specialised roles, academia or were C-suite professionals who had surrounded themselves with experts and peers of either a similar mindset to their own or among people far beyond their abilities. This positioning forced them to articulate their thoughts at an extreme level in comparison to the average talker. Further still, in almost all instances, these affluent communicators expressed a general disdain for long periods of non-productive small-talk and instead chose to use their communication skills to articulate their thoughts to both themselves and others in effort to achieve goals, comprehend complex emotions and work towards greater self-mastery. They spoke like immortals.

In comparison, those who had compounded a carefree attitude to speech and thought soon found that when called to clearly articulate their feelings and opinions, they were unable to do so. Further questioning showed a similarly common theme; lacking the ability to articulate their thoughts often hindered them in their ability to define goals, progress in their careers and conduct rigorous self-introspection. They spoke like mortals. The simple change to be made was the articulation of their thoughts.

Admittedly, this study was small in size and it lacked the grand scale afforded to great investigations of national discourse. Yet, it showed that a majority still suffered from difficulties in articulating their thoughts. Therefore, one has to wonder, what then of the population at large? Why the importance of mentioning it in this book?

I would propose you need only open your ears to answer both questions. It is easy to hear how many take a lackadaisical approach with their words and thoughts. How often have you heard people spiel something nonsensical, give an opinion on a topic they clearly have no knowledge of, speak without thinking, begin a sentence only to suddenly switch to another or struggle to define how they feel or what they saw? In any other ability or skill, this half-hearted approach would not be accepted. Why then do we accept it in something we do every day – speak?

Perhaps society accepts this weakness from ourselves and others because speech is a gift granted to almost all at birth. Speech is free. Almost everyone has a voice. Perhaps it is therefore assumed much as one does not need lessons explaining how to see, one should not need lessons explaining how to think or speak.

I disagree. We should be instructed on how to speak our distinct thoughts from an early age. How often have you heard an adult answer for a child, who if given the chance would be capable of expressing itself? How often has your boss spoken for your 'best interests' when they were anything but? How often have politicians ignored the democratic votes of the people and decided they had the wisdom to rule? It is empowering to both the mind and liberating to the soul to speak for ourselves, to demand reform and to build great things.

Only a hundred years ago schooling concerning grammar, logic and rhetoric, the paraphernalia for the self, were seen as the tools for world builders to be used to free slaves, establish democracies and topple titans – and as with many of humanities gifts, sadly the opposite. But now, this schooling is the domain of the elite, accessible only to those of near noble birth, privilege or extreme wealth who have more recently used them for oppression rather than enlightenment. Such circles deemed you were to be spoken for, not spoken with.

The founding father of McDonalds, Ray Kroc once said "*while formal schooling is an important advantage, it is not a guarantee of success nor is its absence a fatal handicap"*. Yet, in the realm of power, every opportunity counts.

Perhaps it is easily understood why elites have removed such ideas from the public curriculum. The idea of teaching an entire population how to think critically, logically and speak with commanding force would be a danger to those who saw the uprisings of previous generations as a threat to their status quo. *Small talk is called so, because it results in small ideas.*

However, what if a lack of articulate thought and speech among the general population isn't some grand conspiracy? Why then is it so frequent? Why do so many do it? Probably because it's easy. Talking freely at the base levels of mindless repetition uses little mental energy. Relying upon recital of accepted truisms rather than engaging in creative thought is economical. Accepting things as they are saves one from discomfort. Creativity is exhausting and uncomfortable until one has rendered it a habit.

Yet, even if there is no grand conspiracy to keep minds small, this overreliance on comfort can damage your ability to communicate well. Much as weeds need neither fertiliser nor optimum conditions to grow and instead flourish under any circumstances, mental weeds are the same. They will sap the life from all other areas if not replaced with a vibrant garden of creative thought.

What then is one to do when they wish their communication to be as cultivated as a rose garden, and find it only full of thorns and thistles?

First and foremost - adopt the mindset of the immortal by avoiding mundane, mindless chatter. Deep conversation leads to deep thoughts. If you are conversing on a topic, attempt to use all of your abilities to express your opinions, your knowledge and how you feel. My study has shown even minor laziness in daily conversation can quickly become an insidious poison leading to a stagnation of thought, limitation of vocabulary and an overarching inability to articulate the subtle nuances of the emotions which make us who we are. Articulating your exact thoughts will set you apart from others, because the reality is that few rarely attempt to do so.

Secondly, read more outside of your expertise. In all instances, the articulate speakers in my study were avid readers. They understood a book is far more than a mere collection of words on pages. It is the condensed knowledge of years of study by a mind superior in some way to their own. A single quote could change a life, and one hour's reading a day digesting twenty pages could equate to over seven-thousand pages a year, or thirty volumes. Thirty minds mingling with your own is sure to leave an impact. However, be wary of mere desultory reading. Newspapers and gossip magazines rarely contribute much to your thoughts aside noise, trivia and worry. Much as S. *Quidy* eloquently quipped *"mindless reading is like eating empty carbs"* and it is better to read one book well than to abandon ten.

Finally, watch your company. There will be those who abhor deep thought and intense conversation and will ridicule you for attempting it. Do not allow these people to shackle your mind to their low level, like the observers of shadows in Plato's cave. Instead, you must break free and find others who inspire you. Mindless chatter is often unambitious chatter, it is the acceptance of the norm, the desire to talk trivia rather than devise new triumphs. It is the wearing of one-dimensional glasses coated with lack and limitation which flatten the vision, narrow the mind and leave one unwilling to challenge the status quo. The questions *'why are you here?'*, *'where are you going?'*

and *'what is your purpose in life?'* are all the bane of the mindless talker.

Knowing all of this however is no instant cure. No amount of teaching on how to think or how to speak will bring about changes if you do not put these recommendations into practice during your everyday life. Thankfully, this book does not suggest you attempt to impress everyone with grand, poetic declarations of thought in every utterance. Such an act would be pompous and subject to ridicule. Nor does it suggest you avoid talking unless you have some world-changing idea to share. The sad reality is often, we don't. This book merely suggests that you must become more aware of how you articulate your thoughts to yourself and others. It aims to teach you how to answer that most fundamental of all questions: *'what do you think?'*.

PICTOGRAPHS, PROFANITIES, AND POOR VOCABULARIES

Writing is thinking. To write well is to think clearly. That's why it's so hard.

DAVID MCCULLOUGH

Social media isn't social. An alien race looking at the internet today would be forgiven for thinking half of the population communicate in hieroglyphs. The myriad of pictographs and iconography we use in text messages and emails may be easily understood, but much like mindless chatter, there is a danger in their overuse. Known also as *emoticons* these micro-images are often found alongside text in instant messages, social media sites or emails. The most common emoji would be the smiley face :-) which over the years has lost its nose and evolved to :)

I doubt this needs further explanation. Emoji's have become so ubiquitous they can be found as plush toys in our shops. But surely, emoji's can't be that bad! All they are, are cute little pictures and they each carry a generally easily understood meaning. How can they be dangerous?

Well, that's the thing; they are 'easily understood'. Human beings are masters at finding out how to make things easier for ourselves. We are a simultaneously hardworking and lazy species. Generations will strive towards making life easier for the next. Our greatest scientists, mathematicians and physicists will slave over projects which automate mundane tasks. Engineers have made machines which remove the need for backbreaking labour. Programmers have created apps which reduce our workload. This combination of effort and laziness produces results, yet not all of these changes are good. As my study on mindless chatter has shown, an overreliance on taking the easy route can lead to stagnation. I suspect that it is not that emoji's are damaging per-se, more so that their overuse has damaged the way some think and communicate, because emoji's allow us to become lazy with our thoughts and words. The reality is that when using emoji's, we need not rely upon our minds to compose a thought and then articulate it into words or text. Instead, we can simply post a smiley face to show we are happy, a crying face to show we are sad, or perhaps not really know what to say and choose a picture of a turtle in response to "*how are you?*".

Working with clients who have come to me with complaints of brain fog, word recollection issues and communication skills problems has shown how often an overdependence on emoji use has played its part in gradually entrenching a wider lackadaisical approach to their articulation of thought. When texting family and friends, they are liable to replace a carefully curated set of words with a handful of smiley faces. This, repeated over several years becomes particularly damaging to their ability to communicate. Frequently clients contact me expressing a difficulty in expressing their feelings for their partners in valentines, birthday or Christmas cards. Without the ubiquitous smiley face and heart sign common in texting, they struggle to articulate the love they hold for their partners, parents or children. When challenged to send a text without emoji's some even become angry, as if they have been crippled via the loss of a limb leaving them struggling to write. All over the sake of a yellow smiley face.

This then raises the question; are there other common facets of modern-day life which could cause similar problems? I suspect there are. Similar to the emoji, Facebook instead suggests we 'like' rather than comment. Demanding narrowminded acknowledgement is a most dangerous act which has the potential to replace the liberty of composition and critical thought with blind acceptance. Both extreme-left and right-wing narratives demand the same – one is to agree, never question or speak up. Elsewhere online, Twitter also limits our words; thoughts must be a short quip or a joke, rather than a branching essay. Of course, use of these sites is thankfully not mandatory, but they can pose a problem if they become a regular venue for one's mind to dwell within, without consideration to more nuanced, deeper thought and self-expression.

I do empathise with the younger generations raised with the internet as their library. Although they have the sum of all known knowledge (and nonsense) at their fingertips, why should they become a clear articulator of their thoughts when a mere :) will suffice amongst their peers? Why should they say how they feel if simply pressing 'like' will show they agree and make them part of the crowd? Why should they articulate their thoughts if a selfie or picture of their food, watch or shoes will gain them fleeting influence? For this generation, who are more connected than ever and yet speak less and less, will come the largest struggle in communication skills.

Yet, much like an overindulgence of desultory talk and even if you are not part of the younger generations, if you find you are heavily relying upon either emoji's, the 'like' button or making short one-liners rather than engaging in constructive thought, first remember the damage this may inflict upon your creative way with words. Ask yourself, what exactly is it you wish to communicate? Are your words truly reflective of how you feel? How would an immortal express what you want to say?

Of course, all rules have exceptions. When working with clients on the self-expressed autistic spectrum, they have told me that when communicating with another person, the use of emoji's can help them read between the lines of more nuanced emotions. In these instances, the use of an occasional emoji is acceptable.

If you choose to eschew the emoji, I would also recommend you refrain from swearing. Researchers from the Southern Connecticut State University found "...*use of profanity led to the belief that the profanity user was angrier, less trustworthy, less intelligent, and more nonconformist than the speaker who did not use profanity*".[1] Therefore unless you wish to be seen as angry, untrustworthy, unintelligent and an outsider, the use of foul language may best be relegated to your unuttered subconscious.

In my view, swearing is nothing more than capitulating to the unfettered emotions. True, it is human to feel anger, frustration or vexation, yet much as the stoic must temper their mind, so too must the swearer temper their tongue. To resort to the use of crass language shows the mind has yet to adopt the principles, will and strong resolve which serve to make one virtuous. All language is rich with a wonderous number of words, prose and phrase which can adequately portray how one feels without resorting to profanity. Secondly, you may also never know who is listening. A client once told me they were declined a promotion because their poor language was reflecting negatively upon their company's brand and upsetting a senior partner who held polite language in high regards.

Despite how fashionable it may be for magazines, blogs and certain books to report avid swearers to have a 'higher IQ', I have seldom come across a great articulator who resorts to profanity. Much as *Lamont* (1869) said:

"Whatever fortune may be made by perjury, I believe there never was a man who made a fortune by common swearing. It often appears that men pay for swearing, but it seldom happens that they are paid for it. It is not easy to perceive what honour or credit is connected with it. Does any man receive promotion because he is a notable blusterer? Or is any man advanced to dignity because he is expert at profane swearing? Never. Low must be the character which such impertinence will exalt: high must be the character which such impertinence will not degrade. Inexcusable, therefore, must be the practice which has neither reason nor passion to support it. The drunkard has his cups; the satirist, his revenge; the ambitious man, his preferments; the miser, his gold; but the common swearer has nothing; he is a fool at large, sells his soul for nought, and drudges in the service of the devil gratis. Swearing is void of all plea; it is not the native offspring of the soul, nor interwoven with the texture of the body, nor, anyhow, allied to our frame. For, as Tillotson expresses it, 'Though some men pour out oaths as if they were natural, yet no man was ever born of a swearing constitution.' But it is a custom, a low and a paltry custom, picked up by low and paltry spirits

who have no sense of honour, no regard to decency, but are forced to substitute some rhapsody of nonsense to supply the vacancy of good sense. Hence, the silliness of the practice can only be equalled by the silliness of those who adopt it."[2]

If no profit can be made from their use, if they do not elevate you in your career and if the use of profanities is another form of laziness, why use such words? Is it not a shame to hear a young child repeat the vulgarities of an adult who should know better than to sully the ears of youth? Does it not desensitise our minds to other obscenities? Who knows what the effects are from the ever-increasing amount of improprieties wrought by profane words. *George Washington* (1732 – 1799) an exemplary man if there ever was one, similarly decried swearing even during wartime writing in 1776:

"The General is sorry to be informed that the foolish, and wicked practice of profane cursing and swearing (a vice heretofore little known in an American Army) is growing into fashion; he hopes the officers will, by example, as well as influence, endeavour to check it, and that both they, and the men will reflect, that we can have little hopes of the blessing of Heaven on our Arms, if we insult it by our impiety, and folly; added to this, it is a vice so mean and low, without any temptation, that every man of sense, and character, detests and despises it."

If you must insult, substitute your base bleating for creative 'parliamentary language'. Rather than resort to blasphemy, become creative. Take a lesson from one of England's peers in his suggestion that a notorious, failed casino owner and reality TV star was *'suffering from an acute case of verbal incontinence'*. For an Irish proverb says: *'Profanity is ignorance made audible.'*

A WALKING THESAURUS IS A CONVERSATIONAL TYRANNOSAURUS

Wise is the one who learns to dumb it down.

CURTIS TYRONE JONES

What makes a truly first-class cook? Is it one who can present a magnificent meal fit for a King decorated as an appetising feast for the eyes and a decadent treat for the stomach? Is it perhaps one who can prepare any serving with each vegetable flawlessly sautéed and every cut of meat roasted to mouth-watering perfection? Or is it one who can present the meal with a flair, with fires blazing from the kitchen, a plate decorated with gold leaf and served with culinary flourish? Perhaps. But, I believe a truly great cook is one who can take whatever ingredients they have to hand and combine them together into something satisfying for the soul. Their pantry may be close to empty, the contents of their fridge sparse and their cupboards all but bare, yet with the knowledge of how to best combine their few choices of nourishment, comes a meal which would bring a smile to any waiting diner. To this cook, garnishing, plating and rich flavours are all within reach but, ultimately these flourishes are the domain of the professional chef and of little use to those with humble tastes.

The articulate speaker is much like our aforementioned common cook. They are not always a professional chef with a high-class kitchen. Instead they have well-worn tools and knowledge which serve their purpose. To become an articulate and eloquent speaker you need not have vast archives of archaic or obscure words at your command, nor be able to recite Latin aphorisms and Shakespearian lines at whim. You need neither be a master of rhetoric and persuasion able to rile up the masses and cause a revolution. Instead, to become a fine thought-articulator all you need is the ability to effortlessly use common words, which we all know, in a manner which clearly explains your exact thoughts to both yourself and your listeners.

As shown earlier, my clients already had a ready stock of words to draw upon – they simply instead lacked the ability to articulate those words to express their emotions and opinions. They were much as if a cook had delved into a spice rack haphazardly; the resulting dish was unappetizing. The act of placing the right words in the right order was all that was necessary. Of course, in some instances some did need to expand their library of phrases to overcome impoverished vocabularies and vocal fillers such as "*so, yea, ya' know, like, etc...*" which do little to explain what one is trying to say.

There is nothing wrong with wanting to grow your vocabulary. Learners of a foreign language understand the difference between saying "*excuse me, where is the toilet please?*" and "*toilet, where, please?*". The meaning is conveyed in both instances, but the first is a little more eloquent. Therefore, the following exercises are worth practicing and remember to always speak your thoughts and answers aloud:

- Coining a phrase – take a common turn of phrase such as "*...he's like a fish out of water*" and try to explain the emotional meaning behind it.

- Similarities – Choose an adjective and try to list as many synonyms (similar words) as you can and weave them into your daily speech.

- What does this mean? – Attempt to define a word to someone whose first language isn't English.

- Opposites – Choose a word at random and then name its antonym (opposite meaning).

- Rhyme Time – Compose a rhyming poem.

- Welcome to Earth – Imagine you had to describe something so basic you might never otherwise verbalize it, such as the word 'the', to an alien. Be especially careful with your words, as you wouldn't want to hopelessly confuse your new Little Green Friend.

- 日本語が分かるかー If you speak a second language, try to translate emotionally charged poetry or writing from one language to the other.

However, in this practice to expand your lexicon be wary of becoming one of those who relish in peppering their daily phrases with lots of obscure words, for they are often seen as a boor by their peers. These are the people who rather than use simple language, such as the word *protective*, instead use the terms *antimacassar, bandobast* or *cosset*. This use of obscure terminology seems to give them a sense of superiority and grandiosity over their fellow speakers. However, often their use of obscure words is incorrect and ultimately causes their speeches to be misunderstood, leaving them seen as aloof or misinformed. In reality, there is no shame to be found in communicating in simple words when the situation demands so. Gandhi's wisdom of *"you must be the change that you want to see in the world"* showed how sometimes you don't need to use 'big words' to make a great impact.

COMMUNICATION SKILLS VERSUS ARTICULATION SKILLS

If you can't communicate and talk to other people and get across your ideas, you're giving up your potential.

WARREN BUFFET

Most books on communication skills teach people how to speak well with others. However, as this book teaches you how to talk to yourself, what then is the difference between 'communication skills' and 'thought-articulation' given how closely they align?

The term 'communication skills' contains an enormous branch of topics. It comprises of the ability to communicate well with others via the reading of body language, the mirroring of metaphors or the simple act of smiling. An individual with strong communication skills could also be someone who is a keen conversationalist and intense listener, who can effortlessly weave stories which inspire, teach or enthral. Someone with strong communication skills may have a high emotional intelligence and be able to empathise with others and have the ability to charm with their confident charisma.

A book on communication skills is liable to teach you to agree with another person whenever possible, to feed their ego, never one-up their stories and help the other fellow to like themselves a little better. Such recommendations are of course beneficial to improving interpersonal relationships, but they regularly fail to note that *you cannot become a skilled communicator with others if you are unable to communicate well with yourself.* I believe well-articulated self-talk is vitally important to personal growth. Understanding your thoughts, ideals and driving internal forces is crucial for gaining an understanding of the necessary areas which must be improved for further self-mastery. If you cannot express and explain your thoughts to yourself, then you cannot express and explain said thoughts to another.

As with all skills, there are those who have achieved fame and fortune thanks to the development of their mastery in their chosen field. However, given almost everyone can speak it should be an area of paramount importance to become more articulate. I say this, because there are those I have tutored who without such efforts would have remained mute and penniless. Years ago, I received an email from one of these people, she was a distraught young woman, who explained she was applying to university in effort to escape her unfulfilling job as a checkout-clerk. During her first lesson, I asked her why she was in such distress, she replied (verbatim):

"Urr... I'm always told that I'm not thinking straight, because I just- Urr... I just want to get better at talking, because I feel that I'm always- *Sigh* You know when you don't know what to say, and you meet someone who does and it's just-? Oh, and before I

tell you that- err... when I was younger I was never any good at-
well, nothing bad happened but, it's important now because
everyone tells me, well not everyone, but what I try to do now is
that- oh and don't get me wrong, I don't think they are being
mean, it's just- I guess I just want to get better, you know?"

What I heard from this young woman were the words of
someone who struggled to explain her emotions and feelings.
She felt them, but couldn't articulate them. Sadly, the mind's
thoughts do not present themselves in a sequential order.
Instead they are like the passing of innumerable fleeting clouds
twisted by the wind and ever changing in their shape. If one has
unorganized thoughts, it leads to unorganized speech.
Unorganized speech leads to stumbling, stuttering and constant
repetition for the sake of explanation.

In her mind, she felt as if she had a multitude of problems and
with each welling up of emotional turmoil her inner dialogue
demanded attention; each thought pushing and elbowing its
way past the other. Her capitulation to consistent interruption
was the result of repeated circumstance.

Yet, in reality she had but two problems: a lack of structure to
her thoughts and an inability to complete a thought without
other, newer thoughts intruding and derailing her speech. The
lack of structure manifested itself as an inability to speak with a
specific end in mind. The constant permitting of her
emotionally charged inner-dialogue to interrupt her speech, like
an ouroboros gnawing at its own tail, resulted in a perpetual
loop of interruption of unclear communication. Although we
wish thoughts would arrive one by one, like a wizened hermit
walking out of the wilderness with a glimmer of condensed
insight, instead they arrive suddenly, like a cavalcade of frothing

barbarians charging over the hills of our mind leaving a myriad of stray, fragmented footprints upon our grey matter which confuse and confound. Learning to discipline and organise this horde is the only way to turn our myriad of thoughts to our benefit.

Upon prompting her to answer more simplistic questions, I discovered she had no issues with making friends or socialising. However, when socialising she often spoke with little intention in mind. When prompted to speak her mind on a passion of hers she mentioned how she enjoyed painting but could not say why, because she enjoyed it on an emotional level, but was unprepared to express and share this sensation with others in linguistic form.

Thankfully, after teaching her the material contained in this book, I am happy to say this once near-incomprehensible communicator has since graduated with a Bachelor's Degree in Business Management with First Class Honours and is enjoying life, overseeing a small team in a respectable company.

Yet, I am sure you know of many in a similar position who communicate like this. Maybe you suffer from such instances yourself? It is only from persistent practice and effort that one improves. True, there is more to competent articulation skills than just being able to give a coherent answer, but it could be argued that being able to give a coherent answer is the foundation of articulation skills. If an answer is incoherent, it cannot be understood and if you cannot be understood, you cannot relate with other minds.

Therefore, your single most valuable asset is your *mind*. Everything else in your body you can probably find in a pig or a horse, but it is your mind which makes you so. Without an ability to think clearly all other talents fall utterly short.

Without clear thought there is no ability to organise, without organisation there cannot be efficient action and without efficient action there cannot be regular progress.

There is no way to inform others of your talent without first having the ability to express it.

HOW PUBLIC SPEAKING MAY BRING
YOU WEALTH

If I went back to college again, I'd concentrate on two areas: learning to write and to speak before an audience. Nothing in life is more important than the ability to communicate effectively.

GERALD R. FORD

In 2007 I experienced my first major life failure at a London networking seminar. At the time, I had hoped to establish a small-business licensing Japanese manga to be translated and published for readers in the Western-world. It was a large dream, one before its time that required to my estimate no less than three hundred-thousand pounds of funding. I had less than a thousand to my name.

Dressed in an off-the-peg suit, I remember sitting down in a crowd of adults mostly three times my age and feeling diminutive, awed by the luxurious wealth on display around me.

Patek Philippe watches glinted in the spotlights, Gucci scarves draped like weightless wisps around the necks of models and Tiffany diamond dusted slabs sparkled around the fingers of the investors sat beside me. The technology types wore a t-shirt and jeans.

At the stage sat four speakers, each sharing their own viewpoints on how to best invest, how to overcome failure and thoughts on taking risks. They had incredible confidence and a wonderous ability to articulate their ideas. During the lulls between discussions, the attendees besides me talked in telephone numbers: calls of six and seven figure business deals and of plans for multinational expansion. In comparison, at barely 18 I had no collateral for a loan, no business experience, nothing but an idea. However, I was determined to put myself into this uncomfortable situation to learn how things worked in the 'adult world'.

Perhaps I did not seriously consider I would find funding, but I hoped to at least forge one connection, to find one person whom I could learn from or understand. But for that, I needed to communicate my dream. Sadly, what I had not considered to be a problem, was the way I articulated myself.

Although I was fortunate enough to attend school, it was a poor one which cared not for its students. After one bully rammed my bloodied head repeatedly against a wooden staircase and another gored a fountain pen into my back, the resulting fear of attending the grounds left me like a skittish animal. I did anything possible in effort to be expelled for my own safety. Unfortunately, much to my dismay I was not expelled. Instead after yet another episode of battery by self-defence I would be punished to spend the next four years sat alone in a long-forgotten room and being told to "copy from the dictionary".

Free from the horrors of the classroom and the two bullies sat either side of me, I would forego the tiresome task of copying and instead spend the remaining time in near total isolation, wistfully staring out of the window, reading books in the library and hiding in the gymnasium whenever the bells rang.

I am sure you can imagine I was hardly the socialite or competent communicator. At the time however, I thought everything was fine. I assumed I would be able to articulate my thoughts, I had little trouble feeling the emotions which arose from them. Yet in reality when speaking to others, my phrases were halting, my words were poorly chosen and my thoughts were misconstrued. For all intents and purposes, whenever I opened my mouth the words which followed were awkward, inarticulate or woefully unclear.

Yet, here I was surrounded by millionaires, ready to try my best. As the investors took to the floor to mingle amongst each other, it was only then I realised I was out of my depth. When asked questions about my business idea I was as deft with my words as a trapeze artist would be if their limbs had been encased in concrete. It was monumentally embarrassing and eventually I would alienate myself from the entire crowd.

Yet, as I stood outside the circle of influence growing lonelier and lonelier, I could not help to notice how the crowd circled slowly, gradually and almost naturally around those same four articulate speakers who had come to take the stage. It seemed as if they were magnetised, drawing the attention of everyone towards them.

Later I would come to realise the power of what is called the 'stage effect'. Those who had taken the stage were memorable, whereas everyone else who had merely offered business cards were forgettable. Contacting those who had been sympathetic enough to humour me quickly showed how influential I was; I had left neither impact nor offered value. I had been forgotten and rightly so. However, in comparison, those who were invited to talk had shown others their lucidity of thought and eloquence of words and thus became the immediate centres of attention. By taking the stage, they had strategically placed themselves in positions which no business-card or chance meeting could ever overtake. Their bravery and deft-articulation had set them apart from the hundreds of others, which in turn had rewarded them handsomely. It had given them influence. It had given them power. It had turned them from an amateur to an expert. At that moment, they were able to command attention, all for the sake of a few well-chosen words built upon the back of their expertise.

This then raises the question, could you do this with the skills you have now? You need not be a wealthy investor or expert in your field. In truth, no one on a stage knows everything. None of those speakers were the supreme masters of their fields. Each had their own personal weaknesses or questions which they referred to another. None of them were ashamed of saying '*I don't know, but I'll try my best to find out*'.

Ask yourself; what could you share with an audience? What knowledge do you have which sets you apart from others? Is there an experience you could share which if told well would cause others to listen and learn? Such events are electrifying to the soul and add a hefty weight to the wallet. It is little wonder public speaking is the world's highest paid profession. Motivational speakers charge between £5,000 to £25,000 ($7,000 to $35,000) per speech and give around 50 - 100 of them a year. *Boris Johnson* was said to charge £40,000 ($55,000) for a 15 minute after dinner speech, which was reported to be the same speech each and every time.[1] Renown economists, politicians or business magnates usually charge between £100,000 to £450,000 ($140,000 to $625,000) per speech on the corporate circuit. *Bill* and *Hilary Clinton* were reported to have made a total of £110 million ($153 million) in speeches from 2001 to 2015.[2]

Therefore, I ask you to imagine the potential future You who is a capable communicator, effortlessly able to articulate your thoughts, because in that moment, people will be listening. They will be interested. You will have become too adept with your words to ignore. Your influence will grow with each day. Your power and persuasion over people will be used for good. You will become the person who others admire.

Of course, for most the centre stage is an uncomfortable place to be. Similarly, it cannot be ignored that your comfort zone is your income zone. To be comfortable is to stagnate. Had I dedicated my earlier years to self-instruction, to teaching myself how to speak, how to think and how to grow I would have probably met with more fortune and saved myself many years of struggle. The reality is self-instruction, books, clarity of thought and clear speech are the great economic levellers, because they allow for you to communicate with others at levels once unimaginable.

Self-instruction though its myriad of forms has the possibility to transform your life for the better or worse, depending on what you choose to invest in. Some may choose to practice pseudoscience whilst others choose to study science. Others may choose to think upon the mysterious whilst their counterparts master the basics.

However, no matter what you learn, you will always come across a familiarity; that much as every game we play has its own rules which must be abided by, much as societies have their obligations which must be met and much as industry has its regulations which must be followed, attempting to avoid any of these requirements often leads to ruin. Similarly, each social group has its own particular way of speaking to its members and my clients have found it is often those groups which offer the greatest income, demand the utmost thought-articulation skill when communicating in private or public. Ask yourself, what social circles are you part of, or are aiming to join, which would require both elevated level of thought and eloquence? If you cannot find any, you may wish to, because much like life, it is difficult to grow your skills if you do not know where to start.

Importantly, it is almost impossible to talk about public speaking without touching on the right to free speech. I doubt you can imagine a life without free speech, because it is so engrained into our society, but I know one person who can – an escapee of the North Korean regime who I met several years ago.

The horrors which the captives of the *Kim* dictatorship find themselves facing can barely be put into words. It would be uncouth to try. Sadly, our mass media revels in portraying North Koreans as stereotypical cartoon villains who will lay down their lives for the Kim regime, but in reality, this isn't so. These people are human just like you and I. Human beings who experience more suffering than many of us can comprehend; I do not say this lightly, for I do not imagine any of us have spent half a decade eating nothing but grass and insects.

Despite what you may read, not all North Koreans are brainwashed slaves, but in a place under Juche rule, one can only do as they are told. In North Korea, the elites speak at the people, not for them. There is no democracy, no counter opinion, no freedom of expression. It is heretical, in the religious sense to express one's opinion or attempt free speech - death by hanging is viewed as merciful in comparison to the decades of forced-labour which awaits those foolish enough to think otherwise.

In this state, Children are taught the Kim family is omniscient, that he is a literal God who can read their every thought. Family members are pushed to report their own kin; accidentally criticising the state or expressing disdain for the annual quarter pound of rotten meat upon the most sacred of days, the leader's birthday, leads to abduction by the less-than-secret police.

Who can comprehend the horrors of people who are taught their entire lives that literal cannibals are waiting for them outside the gate and yet that their state alone is the strongest, most advanced and greatest nation on earth? Under such repression, who would dare use freedom of speech to object?

Disenfranchised, the concept of a unionised voice, suffrage or human rights is unconceivable for these people. Religious and class indoctrination from birth has forced generations to accept their position in life as being ordained by a fate woven by the Kim godhood. To many, their roll in life was decided decades past alongside wartime strategy; branded as human capital necessary to be mobilised for war at a moment's notice. To the dictators, these people are naught but an insignificant mote of existence, a fleeting slave of time to be ground to dust under the impossible demands made by the state which profits inconceivably upon their silent suffering. In this place, life does not go on, death goes on and nothing changes. This is a world without free speech.

It may now be apparent to you that I hold a strong disdain for societies which fail to give freedom and liberties to men, women and children. In my view, much as declared upon in the Human Bill of Rights, the right to self-educate and speak freely is paramount. Yet societies still exist today, unfettered in their usurping the rights and liberties from once free people, robbing them of the right to free speech.

It cannot be ignored how in dictatorships and Communist states, freedom of speech is one of the first human rights to be suppressed. This is because freedom of speech is the most powerful form of non-violent protest. It empowers humanity by allowing for the expression and sharing of ideas. It fights for change and grants liberties upon the oppressed. It prevents stagnation and in its place calls for growth. It gives the world a free press so that democracies may flourish and offenders be held accountable. It allows for the discovery of truth and the debunking of propaganda. Yet, it is not absolute. Freedom of speech has and will continue to be misused. It has been used to broadcast intolerance and incite violence. It has been used to spread lies and deceit. But, despite this misuse, freedom of speech must be protected.

Freedom of speech has the ability to transform the world around you – for good or evil. In less grandiose settings, the mere effort of sharing your true thoughts in a one to one meeting has the ability to propagate ideas into the minds of your listener, as no thought can ever be influential if it is not shared with others or acted upon. However, you may hesitate at this notion, perhaps thinking that your own ideas are not ground-breaking enough to be worthy of merit, but I ask you to reconsider. Public speaking is much more than standing on a stage before your peers, it is the ability to share your views with others in an informal setting, it is having the freedom to speak to strangers or network outside of your social circle. It increases your ability to think rapidly and critically - for there is nothing more taxing than to be called to speak without preparation. It puts you forward for promotion by shining braver than your peers, granting you increased wealth and prestige. It allows you to be introspective, to question your thoughts and discover new avenues of interest.

You can be stripped of all your assets, lose your friends, colleagues and memberships, but your voice cannot be tamed by force – except by death itself.

CHAPTER 2

DISPELLING GENIUS

Genius, that power which dazzles mortal eyes, is oft but perseverance in disguise.

ORISON SWETT MARDEN

Over two-hundred years ago a French doctor once taunted the great self-made poet, man of letters and Bishop of Nîmes, *Esprit Fléchier*, regarding the wretched poverty of his youth. Fléchier is said to have replied; *"if you had been born and lived in the same condition as I, devoid of all worldly means and academy, you would still be a maker of candles toiling by the lamplight!"*.[1] His and many other similar stories show how with effort, anyone can achieve practically anything. Look around you – everything manmade that you can see began as nothing more than a thought, an electrical impulse in some squishy grey matter. It was action, repeated action which brought it into existence rather than innate 'genius'.

Yet, I have worked with a great many clients who upon being tasked with thought-articulation have initially protested and claimed it was something that could only be achieved by those who could think on their feet and is impossible for them to learn. The usual excuse was to reference their poor academic marks or grades awarded decades prior, as if those marks had been a branding to be carried with them, unchanging, throughout their entire life. After a little goading (and a reminder they were now paying me to complain rather than change their ways) they eventually succeeded.

It does not take any level of genius to become an eloquent thought-articulator – it merely takes practice. Passionate and skilful thought-articulation and extemporaneous speech is a learned skill. No baby is born able to talk. It can only scream. Yet, years later it may hold millions spellbound by a wonderous choice of words and poignant phrase.

Perhaps though prior to purchasing this book you have listened to or read the speeches of great orators and been left in awe at their poetic use of prose, metaphor and aphorism; only to become disenchanted and feel as if such titanic skill is beyond your grasp.

Perhaps you read the word 'genius' describing their skill, further cementing the idea that such brilliance is beyond your abilities. I must protest such a mindset. To claim that 'innate genius' is the only avenue to excellence is foolish, and such a self-limiting belief will act only as an excuse from committing to the responsibility of earnest practice, diligence and conscious thought. In reality, any quality you admire in others can be imitated until it is internalized. It is the result of private practice, not inborn talent which shall lead to others one day ascribing you as a similar titan of the mind and even among those rare motes of human prodigy is the same requirement to abide by the means and rules of study which we humble can benefit from.

The great extempore speaker and politician *Disraeli the Elder* was a thought-articulator. He believed that success was only brought to the front by the repeated hammering of blows on a singular topic like the blacksmith at the forge. He believed that even those with a weak mind, like a blacksmith without a fire, could eventually hammer any metal into whatever shape he should desire.

Often those 'great minds' who have moved the world were not those of genius, they were minds of singular focus, untiring commitment and sheer indefatigable will.

Genius often talks of 'standing on the shoulders of giants', yet fails to admit it once sat first at their feet learning how to rise up. Thought-articulation is the same, no baby is born a grand orator able to declaim before a crowd. They first babble and stutter, confound their audiences with their gurgling and in later life still struggle to express how they feel. Yet, through perseverance the babe eventually grows to become the *Lincoln, Earhart, Churchill, Kennedy* or any other great speaker who you may admire. Yes, some have advantages over others, but all must practice.

Yet, even in our modern times you will still find the antiquated idea that 'great minds are born rather than made' and that 'human pedigree is a matter of proper breeding'. Some people will tell you eloquent writing, speaking and a great many other talents cannot be learned, because they are the sole domain of those stemming from the loins of 'pure bloods'. This is nonsense. Sadly, these notions are still in existence in the highest echelons of our governments, propagated down to the people. This ideal of innate eminence is likely a Victorian workhouse relic which aimed to subdue the common person into subordinance, remaining shackled and unquestioning to their allotted station in life. This antiquated mentality is further reinforced with hackneyed mantras such as *'you can't teach an old dog new tricks'* and public schooling which deprives children of creative thought. Such a mindset need not be part of yours.

Even if you have been subject to such brainwashing, I ask you to examine your life and question; are there not skills you have learnt during adulthood? If so, could you not also learn to become a great thought-articulator, and a similarly great extemporaneous brimming with confidence, charm and charisma?

When I ask these questions to my clients, I am often met with a concerned smile. Many doubt their abilities, especially if they feel they have passed their prime. Doubt robs them of confidence or perhaps they are mired by impostor syndrome. This lands like ash which clouds the mind, occluding thoughts and stifling attempts to act. For that there is only one cure; to act, for it is only the pumping of bellows which fires the furnace.

Many things may hinder you from progress in your studies; a mismanagement of time, a lack of capital or simply impatience; all impede improvement. Worse of all is the disability which often painfully leaves the student struggling behind others. As one well versed with such matters, crippled with a memory disability, I have often wondered how my progress is being obstructed. Yet, I still believe self-instruction is widely possible and both my and my client's careers are evidence of it to be true. Although virtuosos of eidetic memory do exist and their gift for recollection aids their labour, such perfection of memory is not a prerequisite for success. Even those like myself, whose memories are poor to the extent that they can study for hours only to seemingly forget the information the moment the book is closed, find that consistent revisiting of difficult texts lead to gradual familiarity, not unlike how a stranger gradually becomes a friend. No matter what may hold you back, if you persist in articulating your thoughts, you will succeed.

However, improving your articulation skills involves more than just speaking your mind, giving public talks or asking open ended questions. It involves mustering up emotion, conjuring metaphors and using language which resonates with yourself and your listeners and all of this can be learned.

Much as every side of a gem is cut and polished to make it glimmer in the sunlight, each facet of your own developing thought-articulation skills will eventually grant you a radiance which will shine throughout all areas of your life if you work at them. By the effort of practice, you will cultivate within you deep reserves of clarity, poise and answers to pre-meditated questions which can be recalled effortlessly. Eventually, you will elegantly respond, rather than primitively react. Of course, your audience need not be privy to the knowledge that your wisdom, your jokes and your wit are the results of previous effort from learning how to improve your thinking. Instead it shall strike them as innate intelligence, natural talent or perhaps even 'genius'.

It is my fervent belief that any individual, regardless of circumstance, who applies consistent practice to their cause can master any subject no matter how complex. If I did not believe this to be so then I would have wasted my time in writing this book. My clients are not superheroes, geniuses or savants. They are normal people who have elected the option of extraordinary perseverance. They have reached deep down within themselves and found that virtuous pride, wherein one determines that they shall be the master of their own life, rather than a slave to circumstance. They have silenced the clamour of excuses which provides them with an easy retreat, and instead ordered that their dream of speaking well shall be marched forward into reality.

Of course, the art of self-study can be tortuous. One may struggle, fail and retire dejected to mope in a corner overwhelmed and overworked, but should that exhausted soul decide once again to studiously advance in their cause they will ultimately master any topic at hand. A cursory glance through biographies of efforts large and small supports my theory; along all of history we find a regular theme; it was the continuous application of study to overcome once mediocre abilities which led to greatness, rather than innate genius. True, we can find shining stars of genius who illuminate the world with their unsurpassed thoughts and talent, shifting mankind to higher levels of existence which can barely be understood. Yet, such majesty is rare and such merits are unnecessary for the common man; all that is required to become learned is a well-invested hour of reading, study and thought-articulation once per day over a similarly small number of years. Alarmingly, if you read more than one book per year, such devotion makes you more well-read than the average of your peers, a minute act which has the ability to influence your life to degrees unfathomable.

Yet, much as the question Philip asked the Nobleman of Ethiopia, *"Understandest thou what thou readest?"*, be sure to digest what you read. There is no shame in postponing a work if a more elementary introduction is required.

Therefore, always remember that even if you have tried and failed in the past, such reality does not mean your dreams cannot be achieved in the future. You must continue to be a staunch believer, for if you believe something can be done, it is most probably possible. We once said it was impossible to travel to the moon; but we have been there with cars, playing golf. We once said it was impossible to fly, but you can gaze up at the azure and see behemoths in their hundreds trailing across the globe. We once said computers were an impossible task, yet through science we convinced silica and rocks to 'think'. Any skill you see others demonstrate can be learned or mastered by yourself, for in free countries, there is only one who can hold you back – yourself.

It was Les Brown in one of his magnificent, motivational speeches who proclaimed with his grandiose and empowering flair that:

"...the graveyard is the richest place on Earth, because it is here that you will find all the hopes that were never fulfilled, the books that were never written, the songs that were never sung, the inventions that were never shared, the cures that were never discovered, all because someone was too afraid to take that first step, keep with the problem, or determined to carry out their dream. The graveyard is the loneliest place on Earth, for it is here where all the dreams have gone to die."

Still, upon mentioning this to students I am often met with dejected faces. These students quickly inform me in an almost pre-rehearsed manner of some defeat in their youth or in later life. They deliver it as if it such words were a well-weathered rule etched into their body, a shackle holding them bound to the mast of a ship doomed to sail inescapably into a most terrible maelstrom. They reference times when they tried again, again and again to succeed and yet still failed. For such memories, I say the world has been unusually kind to those who it once branded idiots, after they gained success; but it was cruel and bitter towards them whilst they were struggling with failure. It was the oppressive and overbearing despair smothering these misunderstood 'failures' which served to kindle the embers smouldering in their minds. Minds much as your own, for no matter what struggles you may face, with conviction and confidence in success at your cause, you can succeed. You may stumble, you may falter, you may fall down and have to start again, but never belittle yourself. You speak to yourself more than anyone else, so ensure you say empowering things.

The Ancients said 'Know Thyself', but in today's modern world it is imperative you should 'Help Thyself'. Help yourself by taking every opportunity. Help yourself by investing every spare minute in study. Help yourself by filling your mind with thoughts of success, rather than excuses for inaction or failure. If you do not believe success is possible, think of what mankind can overcome and consider your excuse. Think of the former slave, *Frederick Douglas*; a man once shackled and bound to the will of his driver, a man once denied ownership of his body, a man who fought to be free to become a statesman, orator and reformer for the unjust.

What excuse do you have in the modern age with all your rights, with all your opportunities and with all your choices in comparison to these men and women who lacked even the sacred, civil liberties of self-determinism? None at all, because it is not over until you quit.

CAN I REALLY CHANGE HOW I SPEAK?

All the great speakers were bad speakers at first.

RALPH WALDO EMERSON

Alongside being a communication skills coach, I am also a voice actor. In this position, my voice is heard by thousands of people around the world in automated announcements, documentaries or audiobooks, essentially acting as a record of my voice lest I ever become mute again.

Surprisingly to some, most of this work involves using my normal speaking voice, but there are occasional recordings which require me to characterise my voice like those in a cartoon. If you have ever tried to change your voice you may experience what numerous other voice actors have found; it is quite easy to change your voice to a different one, but it is fiendishly difficult to sustain that voice for long periods of time.

This may lead you to believe that it simply isn't possible to change how you speak; you may believe you are too old, you may feel as if your speech is too innate to change. There may even be a more insidious handicap - regularly I hear from clients who are troubled with negative self-talk stemming from being branded an 'idiot' as a child, with the insult spinning like a broken record on repeat in their mind and leaving them feeling as if change is impossible. Yet, working with hundreds of clients has proven to me that *changing how you articulate yourself* is far easier than *sustaining a changed voice*. You could have a terrible voice which is raspy and unpleasant to hear, but if you convey the right words your audience will forgive you.

Improving how you speak will also grant you the ability to articulate the exact truth of your thoughts. Poetry is popular because it spells out the mirrored thoughts others have which they cannot communicate to themselves. By finding this truth, you will be able to elevate your mind to positions of understanding, introspection and virtue which were once a hazy mirage of thoughts. With practice, your mind and speech will be patient in the face of criticism, contraction, or opposition. It will become like a rock on the seabed floor which cares not for the raging storm and crashing waves above.

Unfortunately, when learning of these benefits people often ask me if they can change their thoughts and speech *rapidly*. As a whole, we are incredibly impatient. I have often been asked if one can take some form of supplement, complete an exercise or if there is a 'trick' to great speech. Sadly not.

However, relative to our entire lives we do quickly change how we think and speak. From birth your thoughts and speech have gradually grown much like your body. Whereas once you babbled like a babe, in but a few short years you began to understand rudimentary terminology and could produce simplistic phrases outlining your most basic needs. Later in life you eventually began to understand more complex terminology and gained a sense of self-expression outside the material. In teenage rebellious phases, you may have considered countercultures, maverick ideals or merely engaged in an overuse of profanity as an effort to counteract the demands of others. Yet, in later adulthood one then has the choice of either letting their speech degrade through laziness or grow through constant cultivation.

Clients often tell me that attending a college or university was the most impactful moment in fostering a rapid growth of their speaking skills. Surrounded by superior intellects, they are immersed in a sea of ideas which washes over their mind, new thoughts and philosophies acting as waves making pools which begin to teem with life in their psyche. Yet sadly, in their working life these people often experience what I call a period of *linguo-intellectual stagnation,* as their colleagues, responsibilities and workplaces fail to offer the majesty of great theories, deep conversation or profound learning found in academia. This results in a diminishing level of thought and verbal expression as the once teeming pools of life evaporate, leaving only the dry beds of occupational drudgery. In need of insight, the motivated turn to books, online lectures or debating clubs for guidance and stimulation. Once again immersed in a sea of new ideas, their speech and the comprehension of their native tongue is again elevated in proficiency, granting them an increased level of fluency and lucidity of thought. It is soon realised that such levels of mastery can only be sustained through continued exposure to vitalising conversation and the changing of how one thinks, rather than the changing of the voice.

Therefore, rather than being concerned about changing your voice, your priority should be to change your thoughts by ensuring they are exposed to the elements by thought-articulation, open discussion and deep contemplation.

WHY IS IT DIFFICULT TO CHANGE HOW I SPEAK?

Every speaker has a mouth, an arrangement rather neat.
Sometimes it's filled with wisdom, sometimes it's filled
with feet.

ROBERT ORBEN

You have now learned that it is possible to change the way you speak, but that doesn't mean it's always easy. If someone has ever indicated how often you use a particular word, turn of phrase or vocal filler such as *'umm'* or *'err'* you will quickly find it is quite difficult to unlearn those habits. Although this is not a book on neurology, I feel it is worthwhile to furnish you with a simple explanation of why it can be so fiendishly difficult in the first few weeks to change a habit and why it quickly becomes easier if you persist.

In your mind you have a wonderous thought engraver, who with but one touch of his stylus upon the tablet of your mind is able to leave his mark. With each repeated nick and hammering of this tool these marks grow deeper and cleaner. Each repetition of thought carves a channel, upon which memories can easily be read and recalled. Nothing, aside the destruction of the brain, has shown that these engraved recollections, experiences or habits can be completely forgotten. The mind in its prestigious wealth and respective poverty stores each and every shaving of thought which at any time can be within the ken of consciousness. Such engravings are why the dogmatic Fascist is made, not born. Long and repeated etchings of Fascist thought-channels grew so deep that counter thought could not run in any other direction. By the merits of such singlemindedness logical reasoning fails, mental elasticity perishes and empathy for those not of the similar persuasion is replaced with bigotry and hatred. This is the conclusion for one so engrained in thought which is unquestioning to the status quo. Compare this to the freedom-lover, whose mind is malleable and willing to forego once established tracks in effort of forging new avenues, which bring about goodwill and happiness.

Our engraver's markings are called in scientific circles 'neurons'. These organic electrical channels cause the brain to have conscious or subconscious thoughts. Powered by minute electrical charges, neurons are responsible for almost every action in the human body and therefore extremely energy intensive; to the extent they consume approximately forty percent of our daily calorific intake.

Much as an engraver may fill a finished section with enamel to allow for the grooves to be seen from afar, with each firing of a neuron, the brain wraps the regularly used neurons with a substance called *myelin*. Myelin is best imagined as the insulation covering an electrical cable preventing sparks from branching elsewhere. If a neuron fires to another area of the brain, it may cause unexpected consequences; *synaesthesia* is a prime example, where in rare instances the crossing of neurons causes some people to be able to taste colours, see sounds or hear smells. This crossing of the wires may explain why we have a tradition of lowering the lights at orchestral performances, because some of the earliest composers may have been synthesists who would have demanded a violinist or pianist to '*play a little more blue*'.

Unfortunately, negative speech habits and similar issues are all repeated because the brain has already spent a large amount of energy in wrapping neurons with a substantial myelin sheath. Much as an engraver can choose to ruin a tablet by hammering too deeply, on a survival basis, the brain does not care if the habit we have is detrimental to us. Changing a habit involves spending more energy than is being expended in creating new neurons. When we attempt to change our habits, the brain is displeased by such a sudden demand for new neurons. It was not aware that the old ones were broken, so why fix them? The penny-pinching, spendthrift brain is suspicious of such lavish expenditures. It frets that "*...if we keep that up, we may run out entirely!*" Our brain effectively works against our actions to prevent us from starving to death.

The brain is so energy demanding that chess grandmasters are often at risk of becoming gaunt, skeletal figures in the leadup to a championship due to the sheer amount of calories burned in forging new neurons by thought alone. It is also why those undergoing severe stresses may lose weight despite eating regularly. My clients occasionally experience the same exhaustion during lessons, because I am forcing them to create new neural channels instead of defaulting to old ones - much to the choosy brain's chagrin.

Thankfully, much as an engraver can obtain new tablets to work upon, the brain creates new neurons throughout your entire life and it is possible to change habits in a short amount of time. Nevertheless, the first few weeks are the most frustrating, because your brain is purposefully trying to sabotage you in effort to save energy. Much as an apprentice engraver would fumble with their tools and ruin their practice tablets, so too will you struggle in your initial efforts.

The best thing you can do to aid with this progress is to *practice gratitude* when realising you have made a mistake rather than criticising yourself, because this action aids with motivating you to continue.

Should you continue and push past these initial struggles you will experience a phenomenon which some coin as the moment when 'it just clicked'. This is the moment when the brain has invested the necessary energy in wrapping the newly created neurons in enough myelin to have them become the default pathways for thought – making your progress much easier and more enjoyable. A simple example would be the first time someone attempts to use a keyboard or piano; they initially hen-pick at the keys. Yet, once the neurons have a necessary amount of myelin sheath to become entrenched, the actions become part of subconsciously driven muscle memory requiring no further neurological construction; their fingers begin to glide over and 'tickle the ivories'.

As you practice you will struggle. Yet, with anything you do, your first attempt will always be your worst, but with every other attempt you will improve. Do not become dismayed when challenged to articulate your true thoughts if you stutter, stumble or trip over your own tongue. A baby never learns to walk on its first try, it continues to fall, reassert itself and fall again. Yet one day, it never falls again.

If like a new born babe, words fail to come to your mind, your thoughts are a tangled mess or you sit dumbfounded when attempting to define the most simple of words, it is completely normal, for with competence comes confidence.

IS ELOQUENT SPEECH DIFFERENT FROM A GOLDEN VOICE?

> *Somebody once said I had a face for radio and a voice for newspapers.*
>
> JERRY SPRINGER

Do you remember hearing those golden voiced radio announcers and presenters who graced the airwaves with their silver tongues? Their reassuring tones in moments of crisis or the soft, gentle-spoken melodies of their storytelling charmed millions. Yet, it wasn't only their voice which made them popular, it was what they said.

A great communicator who weaves a wonderous story that enthrals their audience is much like a beautiful piece of music which captivates the listener with its melody. In comparison, a poor communicator is like a child at a piano bashing randomly at the keys. They make some noise, but no matter how hard they try it is rarely pleasant. There are also those with beautiful voices who still leave little impact, for a rich voice may ring in the ears of a listener and please the mind in the moment, but it is of little use if the words fail to resonate inside the mind. This then begs the question; is mastering how you communicate different from cultivating a great voice?

My previous work *Speak and Be Heard* (2019) was a comprehensive textbook of vocal exercises aimed at strengthening the voice in terms of breath support, enunciation, richness of sound and melody. In short, it aimed to give people a golden voice. As a whole, it met with success, with reviewers reporting how by following its teachings they improved the sound of their voice. Yet, a great voice alone will not result in a boon of income, prestige or self-confidence. It is the words chosen which deposit these assets.

When asked by my students how one can learn to communicate well, some expect a lesson on the techniques taught in my previous work. Some expect me to teach them a breathing or vocal technique to leave them with a grand, stentorian voice which pleases the ear, similar to *James Earl Jones's*. What they fail to consider is that a 'great voice' is usually accompanied by a similarly excellent choice of words delivered in an eloquent manner through well-organised thoughts.

I have known many speakers with terrible voices; those which crack, those which pop and those which are riddled with vocal fry, who despite these handicaps have been wondrously articulate communicators and whose minds have granted them astounding fortunes. Bob Dylan is a prime example; his voice was once described as *"a raw, very young, and seemingly untrained voice, frankly nasal, as if sandpaper could sing"* and yet he has found fame, fortune and a Nobel prize for his masterful choice of words.[1]

In reality, to perfect your diction, elocution and richness of tone would only serve to allow an audience to enjoy the *sound* of your words; if you lack the ability to produce a clarity of eloquent *thought*, all utterances would fall short of influencing their mark. Do not become obsessed with cultivating a golden voice, instead focus on improving your thoughts.

Unlike Dylan, one-hit wonders experience a similar paradox; the music they produce is wonderful to listen to in the moment, but it fails to stir the soul and stand the test of time. Therefore, if you believe that only the golden voice of the silver-tongued orator rings true you would be incorrect. Great speakers are made of great thoughts and great thoughts must be articulated well for all to hear.

Yet, this is not to say you can rely upon thought-articulation to appear an expert authority on any topic. I would loathe to advise readers act as the common middle-management or political types who bluster through every speech and say little despite delivering many words. Instead, daily practice should save you from the embarrassment of stumbling over your thoughts, words or having nothing to say when called to speak.

Before we continue however, a brief caveat: it is important you accept that all the teaching in the world will be useless to you without first accepting that success is possible. You must imagine yourself as capable and envision yourself a year from now brimming with confidence, charisma and charm as you finalise yet another successful meeting or conversation thanks to your improved thought-articulation skills. Through your efforts, doors once bolted shut will open for you, people will contact you for interviews rather than you demanding their attention and you will become an influencer rather than a follower.

With improved thoughts and articulation skills, you can out-earn your colleagues, run a successful business or even speak in front of thousands. There is little you cannot accomplish if you demonstrate your capabilities with your improved thought-articulation skills. Further still, as a proficient speaker, your ideas will be sound, your words will be strong and your passion clear for all to see. You will no longer awkwardly present and lecture, instead you will effortlessly converse with each listener who will be transfixed at your every word, mind so synced, they may as well be one – even if they don't agree with you. With renewed precision of thought, coherent ideas will flow effortlessly from your lips as you improvise at will during question and answering. You will leave behind the old you which used to tremble and stutter at the idea of even raising your voice above a whisper and become the best you can be.

Socrates, a figure of profound clarity of thought and speech once said *"all men are sufficiently eloquent in that which they understand"*. Yet, having listened to many a dreary and ineloquent speech given by experts I must disagree with the old master. Unless you know how to communicate your knowledge using well-constructed eloquence (organised thought), your message is merely conveyed into the air; it is unable to rest upon the mind of the listener. Many a professor has attempted to speak pure knowledge, but this, presented plainly, is dry and devoid of life. On the other hand, we see novices attempt to decorate their speech with rhyme, rhythm and rhetoric, but this serves only to create a pleasant melody rather than inform the audience. Impactful speech requires balance of understanding, eloquent prose and a genuine emotional delivery to persuade others by the virtue of intellectual osmosis. Such an art can only be mastered if you first change the way you think, rather than strive towards a golden voice.

YOU DON'T NEED TO SPEAK IN
RECEIVED PRONUNCIATION

Always be yourself and have faith in yourself. Do not go out and look for a successful personality and try to duplicate it.

BRUCE LEE

Years ago, I vividly remember discovering a strange phenomenon whereupon uttering a single word, I was able to change an Englishman's accent in the most unusual of ways.

Sat before me was an imposing ex-coal miner with a voice reminiscent of a whale which had spent a lifetime gargling lava-encrusted rocks from the seabed floor. Thirty years of bellowing to his colleagues behind dynamite, drills and the occasional cave-in had given this gentleman vocal fry with one volume: loud, and one tone: gruff. Having contacted me hoping to subdue his tones to be more suitable for a quiet office environment, this charming, impactful and commanding voice would suddenly become fruity, flowery and near-effeminate the moment I mentioned the concept of '*eloquent speech*'. It was as if I were watching a pantomime performance and he was playing the part of Mrs. Muffet, waiting for a hidden audience to shout "*He's behind you!*" only for him to respond "*Oh no he isn't!*". Strangely, this phenomenon is a common issue especially among English, Indian and American learners and it is one you should also be aware of.

It is my thinking that when introducing the concept of speaking with 'eloquence' to some, they hold a stereotype in their mind which leads to them adopting a speaking style with an unnatural, archaic accent; specifically *Received Pronunciation* (RP). For those who are unaware of this term, it is the antiquated 'posh' British accent as spoken by aristocrats, James Bond villains and the Royal Family.

Interestingly, English and Indian learners mimic received pronunciation whereas American learners lean towards the Transatlantic accent or some faux-English amalgamation. Yet, in my view, such modification is unnecessary. The act of changing your accent to become 'eloquent' is, in my view, the antithesis of eloquence. Eloquence should be the embracing of the most natural, honest self and outlining your true thought-articulation. The Dictionary of Oxford Languages defines eloquence as '*fluent or persuasive speaking or writing*', it makes no note of antiquated accent, longwinded language or pompous polish. Further still, much like this book; it stresses neither any importance on the clarity of enunciation or the richness of a voice. Aim to practice all the exercises in this book and your thought-articulation whilst retaining your unique voice; you need not affect an unnatural accent. True bravery is not leaping from a bungee jump, walking on coals or swinging on a trapeze; those are insignificant compared to the bravery and courage to be yourself.

ANYONE CAN SPEAK WITH PASSION

Be still when you have nothing to say; when genuine passion moves you, say what you've got to say, and say it hot.

D. H. LAWRENCE

Occasionally I have clients who tell me they simply cannot muster the emotion to speak with passion. Yet, there is no better spur to rouse your ability to talk than to defend something you hold close to your heart. Several years ago, I saw such a speech.

Whilst waiting for my turn to use a self-checkout machine in a local shop, before me was a woman in plaid and a man in blue. Walking forward I remember the man in blue placing his few items on the counter and then discreetly beckoning to a nearby member of staff. I would soon learn that the lady waiting behind him was an accused shoplifter, who had supposedly placed a number of small bottles of alcohol inside her coat. Hearing this, the portly security guard strolled into action, with staff slowly walking either side of her whilst another called for a manager. All of a sudden, every eye was on the accused.

Bewildered, flustered and accosted the lady in plaid protested her innocence, emptied her pockets and showed she had nothing but her basket of unpaid goods. Her defence was filled with emotional language, descriptions of innocence and claims that she had done nothing wrong. In her emotional state with no time to prepare, her voice was strained and her talk had made itself. In all intents and purposes, it sounded true. Sadly, the staff, no-doubt having become jaded by the regular occurrence of theft did not believe her. One said they intended to call the police, the other mocking her as she began to break down in tears. As the agonising minute passed I shouted for attention, but it was too late. All of a sudden, the alarm sounded and eyes darted to the door. Persuaded by the keen innocence of the lady in plaid's pleas which had aroused no suspicion of guilt, I had trained my eye elsewhere for but a few seconds and noticed the man who had accused her of theft, was the one who had now bolted out the door, goods unpaid in hand. Having escaped, the staff were then at the mercy of the crowd who had suddenly decided now was a suitable time to defend the poor woman, rather than keep their eyes glued to their phones as they had done only moments prior.

But why reference this memory? Because it shows that anyone, at any time, is capable of speaking on the spur-of-the-moment with passion should they hold a strong enough conviction to do so. Perhaps with the training referenced in this book, this poor lady under duress could have convinced her accusers otherwise.

By this virtue you can hopefully see why passionate speech is important. In this and most every demanding or unforeseen circumstance, passionate speech is elevated from an important tool in your kit to a truly indispensable implement. Who would reject something which can empower them so? Growing levels of multiculturalism and international trade (European withdrawal suicide aside) along with the potential for artificial intelligence freeing millions from mundane jobs, have made it a requirement for each and every individual to have levels of clear, concise and passionate thought-articulation skills. Nowadays, hiring managers demand at least one form of public speaking skill, which will only further increase with the normalisation of remote working and online presentations. It is therefore vitally important you learn how to speak your true thoughts. Now more than ever we need people with the ability to inspire; now more than ever we need people with the ability to lead; now more than ever we need people with the ability to speak well.

Sadly, a common complaint I hear from clients are the words *'I just can't do it'*. These are the people who have gerrymandered their words to satisfy the demands of their supposed superiors; who have internalised their past failures and rendered themselves as verbal cripples. Countless more are held in self-imposed suppression by a fear which gnaws at their mind entrenching paradigms which maliciously claim they are not knowledgeable enough to speak. This lack of faith paralyses them, leaving them as mutes in a world led by talkers.

Yet, paradoxically, I am sure you also know of a colleague who is a walking library of knowledge. This individual, if given enough time, can solve any conundrum, fix any broken system and has probably walked office halls longer than anyone else. Nevertheless, despite their familiarity and knowledge of the topic at hand they are kept relegated to menial work down in some corporate basement. This is not due to a lack of knowledge; instead it stems from an inability to communicate *effectively*. If on the other hand you struggle to express emotion due to a weakness of feeling, consult the exercises on '*How to Express Emotion*' near the end of this book.

In almost all cases, the people who I teach clearly have the knowledge of what to say and insight which has not been considered, but they lack the confidence to share such expertise with others. This can be remedied by fervent practice of the exercises detailed so far and the repeated recitation of the grandest of empowering phrases; '*I can do it.*'

CHAPTER 3

HOW YOU THINK IMPACTS HOW YOU SPEAK

Think like a wise man but communicate in the language of the people.

WILLIAM BUTLER YEATS

There is a paradox with this heading. Some would argue that how you speak impacts how you think. Others would say how you think impacts how you speak. This chicken and egg argument doesn't have a true answer, but the concept behind the statement is important. Let me demonstrate why.

Close your eyes. Think about how you will improve your speaking skills in the future. Do you hear a voice? If you do, this is your internal dialogue and it communicates to you your thoughts, your ideas and your emotions. It guides them, expands them and can limit them. Even those with *aphantasia* a lack of imaginative vision have some form of internal dialogue. It is such an innate part of the human condition that the vocal cords even exhibit *subvocalization*, micro-movements when people engage their internal dialogue. With sensors or lasers, it is even possible to ascertain those movements, to define them and in a way 'read' thoughts.[1]

This raises an important distinction. On the one hand we have self-communication as a pure, unvocalised emotion. These are the raw thoughts, the seeing red when angry or the blinkers limiting one's vision when blinded by love. On the other, we have the translation of emotion into internal dialogue. Pure emotion is base and reactionary, but by giving it voice with internal dialogue and subvocalization it quiets its roaring nature and brings us a step closer to taming it entirely. When reading in silence this desire to 'speak' our internal dialogue aloud is so strong that some can be observed making involuntary micro-movements with their lips, such is the desire to let our thoughts escape into the world around us.

Curiously however, there are some people who have never subvocalised. These are the people who read a book in mental silence and hear no words materialising from the page, nor do they have any form of internal voice. This can be detrimental to thought-articulation if not rectified. Thankfully, it is especially easy to learn how to subvocalize – simply close your mouth and 'speak' in silence by moving air past the vocal cords. The air should exit your nose and you may occasionally make micro-movements with your lips. With this practice, you may begin to hear your voice inside your mind in tandem with these movements of air. However, unlike whispering where an attempt at communicating with others is made, subvocalization is purely a private affair. There should be little to nothing in the way of sound produced. If you are practicing this for the first time you will notice an immediate slowing of your thoughts, which is crucial for reining in the uncontrollable animal nature that is base emotion.

Subvocalization can be a joy to discover, because it breathes life into reading novels, poetry and fiction by granting characters different voices made from your own. Subvocalization also allows for you to begin to translate pure emotional feeling into words - a necessary step towards being an eloquent communicator. If you happen to already have the skill of subvocalization be thankful that much like all other eloquent speakers, you already have the mental tools necessary to succeed.

Regardless of if you can immediately subvocalize or not, you may have come across a common problem – it is easy to *feel* the right answer to a problem, but quite difficult to express it in words. Yet, by finding those words it will quickly help you agree with what all the great wise men and philosophers decreed long ago; *'we become what we think about'*. I mean this not in some esoteric, spiritualistic or metaphysical manner, but more-so in the reality that the way you think relies upon the style in which you speak (or perhaps the way you speak is reliant upon how you think – I'll leave you to ponder aloud on the paradox). Therefore, to become an eloquent and lucid speaker, you require eloquent and lucid thoughts and vice versa.

Is it not curious how a thought can exist in our minds immaterial, and yet once it is translated into the spoken or written word it takes form? How often do you hear people expressing they have struggled to explain how they feel, until someone else asked them to simply write their thoughts down on paper or 'talk to someone' only for the thought to articulate itself? There is a reason speaking your internal dialogue through *talking therapy* is such a powerful technique to heal the mind.

Given the unique nature of the mind, people talk to themselves in a myriad of different manners far in excess of the scope of this book. Therefore, I have summarised six prominent archetypes I have met during my career. In many instances, several of these archetypes can be found in the same person, but identifying your own major archetype is invaluable to your progress to being a clear thought-articulator.

- *Reactives* – The type who rely primarily upon past experiences rather than think with foresight. They often speak with little thought to consequences; these are the people who often make up the ranks of the angry, who fill the prisons and those who speak before they think landing them in trouble. Their words are highly emotionally charged and they often lack an internal dialogue making them the weakest self-articulators.

- *Creatives* – The type who draw upon creative insight to create whimsical responses brimming with metaphor and visual imagery; these are the artists, the deep-thinking philosophers and poets. Their spoken words convey a strong sense of emotion, but are often either verbose due to an attempt to articulate the subtle nuances of what they wish to convey or limited due to indecision. Although an internal dialogue is present, they often struggle to translate their true emotion into linguistic reality.

- *Socialisers* – The type who enjoy socialising and establishing a sense of familiarity within their tribe; these are the networkers, the team workers and the self-sacrificers. Although they may not have a particularly strong internal dialogue, their empathetic nature, strong listening skills and desire for belonging often allow them to articulate the thoughts of others better than their own.

- *Troubleshooters* – The type who, like military strategists armed with a panoply of problem-solving skills, try to consider every variable and speak in logical terms; these are the mathematicians, the inventors and the investors. Their attempt to provide structure to the world leads them to speaking mostly in technical language which can often be misunderstood. Their internal dialogue is strong and guided less by emotion and more by rationality.

- *Leaders* – The type who use their well-defined goals to persuade others to follow in their footsteps; these are the CEO's, the thought pioneers and visionaries. Their internal-dialogue is well established leading to strong articulation skills, allowing them to convince others of the merits of their ideas. However, they can often be headstrong, lacking in empathy and occasionally manipulative if they are too confident that the end justifies the means.

- *Loopers* – The type who worry and ruminate till exhaustion; these are the anxious, the indecisive and those with a negative outlook on life; their internal dialogue is so strong that it has overpowered their ability to cease their thoughts, leading to near-neurotic behaviour. Despite having the strongest of internal dialogues, it is centred around asking 'why' questions which probe for problems, rather than 'what' questions which seek opportunities.

Learning which major archetype you align with will aid with identifying how you self-articulate. None of these archetypes is perfect and rarely can only one be found in one person, because each has its use in the right moment. Each archetype relies upon their internal dialogue to solve problems and express themselves. Crucially then, each archetype is both guided and limited by their level of internal dialogue.

Knowing this, despite having thought and communicated internally almost all your life in both private and public, have you considered the restrictions placed upon your abilities if you are unable to examine and explain yourself?

If not, do not be alarmed. I say this, because I have met with hundreds of successful, intelligent and wealthy clients from each archetype who tell me the same tired words of; *'I know what I want to say, I just don't know how to say it'*. Perpetually stuck, their knowledge of 'what to say' is limited to experiencing glimmers of passing emotion rather than solidified linguistic expression. Years of being unable to translate those transient, ephemeral emotions into the spoken word often makes them feel as if they are ignorant.

In reality this is not the case – it merely means they are experiencing a persistent weakness of word recollection and a struggle to articulate their emotions. Much as one would struggle in battle without soldiers at their command, so too one would struggle in conversation and thought without a ready stock of ideas and an ample vocabulary.

As mentioned earlier, to overcome a weakness of internal-dialogue I would stray away from suggesting you are expected to become a walking dictionary furnishing each sentence with archaic terminology and quotation. I would also disavow the notion that you need translate *every* thought you have, because such an exercise would most probably cause madness. Instead, aim to subvocalize *creative* thoughts such as mulling over personal ideals, self-introspective investigation or the machinations of your mind when processing surprising new information. This is best achieved by cultivating a strong command of the most regularly used words in your language and industry using the previously outlined exercises and the exercises which will follow.

Much as it is not necessary to turn over an entire library to gain a basic knowledge of a subject, you need not know every word coined by mankind. It is the strength in recalling and weaving the most commonly used words which will allow you to communicate your thoughts and abilities effortlessly with your audience. If you find a word to be on the tip of your tongue, once it comes to the fore attempt to make several short sentences using it. Should you wish to add a sprinkling of flourish or rhetoric for artistic effect consult the examples which will follow shortly.

For further improvement, take note to the organisation of your thoughts. If our thoughts were like pearls which glistened with their multitude of insights, it would be better to string them in a straight line so each could be studied, rather than heaping them upon a table with each hiding the other. Sadly, many present their thoughts to others in a disorganised manner, much like a cuttlefish which when backed into a corner releases a torrent of ink to confound its enemies.

Your thoughts must therefore *begin with an end in mind*. People who fail to communicate with an end in mind do so because they are both grappling with extraneous thoughts and explaining their ideas to themselves rather than to their listener. Ensuring not to 'loop back' to interrupt the recanting of a tale with the words '...*Oh, before I tell you that, let me tell you...*' is something to look out for.

With regular and committed practice to thought-articulation, you can grant yourself speaking skills once unimaginable and for those with little self-confidence, I ask you this; if others can learn how to think and speak well, why can't you? What is holding you back, if not yourself?

THOUGHTS TO THINK ALOUD

Most of the mistakes in thinking are inadequacies of perception rather than mistakes of logic.

EDWARD DE BONO

When speaking with clients for the first time, one of the initial tasks I have them face are logic puzzles known as 'syllogisms'. Supposedly created by Aristotle, these puzzles require the thinker to use logical reasoning to ascertain the correct answer. During a session, the logical reasoning the client uses isn't that important, more-so I instruct them to think aloud, allowing me to listen to how the client articulates their inner-dialogue, helping me also ascertain their personality archetype.

When solving these it is important to read and answer the puzzles aloud, because this will help demonstrate the difference between an *emotional feeling* of something being true or false, compared to a linguistically well-articulated thought.

Gold, Silver and Copper melt easily.
They are metals,
Therefore; all metals melt easily.

'Mouse' is a monosyllable,
A mouse eats cheese
Therefore; a monosyllable eats cheese.

Nothing is better than wisdom,
Dry bread is better than nothing.
Therefore; dry bread is better than
      wisdom.

I then ask them to answer questions which challenge their definition and consideration skills such as:

- What is the difference between *think* and *guess?*

- Is it better to be *doubtful* or *faithful?*

- How long is *a moment in time?*

I then ask them to explain their thoughts concerning abstract ideas:

- Is it better to write quickly by hand or slowly by computer?

- Does an image seen in the mind exist in 2D or 3D space?

- Is the colour green I see the same as the colour green you see?

When working through these exercises, especially the abstract which have no exact answer, one of the more common responses I hear clients saying are statements such as: "...*Yes, that makes sense because... wait no... maybe it's... I don't know? Oh wait, because of...*". These utterances are important, because if their thoughts had not been articulated aloud such emotional confusion would have potentially led to their minds simply accepting the emotion as *frustration* – leaving them unwilling to continue the task or as *acceptance* – causing them to give the wrong answer.

Furthermore, by articulating the thoughts aloud, it forces their mind to grapple with creating logical sentence structures which are devoid of emotion. If you find yourself doing this, do not dismay; as long as you continue your attempt to articulate your thoughts rather than slipping into silence, you are making progress.

Try the exercises above and note your responses, if you suddenly changed your opinion after verbalised introspection you will quickly see how beneficial speaking your thoughts aloud can be.

Another useful exercise is to translate the works of some great author into your own words. Take up any book from your shelf written by an expert, read a sentence, the more simple the better and then summarise it. Move then to the next few sentences and translate the meaning into your own words using a pen if necessary to summarise your thoughts into bullet points which can be expanded upon in extemporised speech. Eventually you will be able to explain entire paragraphs, granting you a depth of understanding. With each effort in saying these thoughts aloud you not only develop your understanding of the text, but also add a stock of ideas to be drawn from your mind.

The summarising of what you read and then expanding upon such notes with extemporaneous speech is monumentally beneficial. With the exception of *thought-articulation*, I have not found another exercise which works so well in both preparing the mind and cultivating a unique sense of spoken style.

STRUGGLING TO ARTICULATE YOUR THOUGHTS MAY BE BY DESIGN

I think there are two ways in which people are controlled. First of all, frighten people and secondly, demoralise them. An educated, healthy and confident nation is harder to govern.

TONY BENN

Earlier, I mentioned how unrestrained mindless chatter is damaging to your ability to communicate. You may have also found the previous exercises challenging. But what if your education has purposely sabotaged your mind to ensure you struggle in being articulate with your thoughts and words - for someone else's benefit?

There are a great many books such as *Sinclair's The Jungle, Hugo's Les Misérables* and *H. G. Wells' The Time Machine* which portray a struggle between an inarticulate, oppressed working class and a silver-tongued, ennobled elite. Have you ever wondered why? Similarly, why is it that some struggle to communicate even the simplest of ideas whereas others explain complex theories with ease? Why are some dazzling storytellers whereas others fade in the limelight? Why do communication and persuasion often appear to be an unfair contest between the rich and the poor?

In this section, I don't talk of inborn advantages such as a photographic memory, cavernous lungs or attractive features. Nor do I talk of those who have studied hard throughout their careers at great expense to their families and social life to learn their craft. I ask you to think of those who perform a little too flawlessly, those whose answers are a little too polished and those who strike like a fake among the real. The rabble-rousers, the populists, the double-breasted 'floccinaucinihilipilification' referencing elite – who are generally never on the side of the working man and woman. Why are these people so convincing to some and so transparent to others?

The answer probably lies in your youth. Do you remember studying lessons on debating techniques, rhetoric and poetic eloquence between science and mathematics? No? Perhaps you had lessons on value investing, day trading speculation, and portfolio diversification. Not those, either? The sons and daughters of polite society do. It is why if a member of the working class breaks through these barriers they are fetishized for their apparent 'authenticity'.

Only a hundred years ago if born to wealthy parents, a student would have studied the speeches of the master orators *Cicero, Demosthenes, Gladstone* and *Disraeli*. That same student would have been called upon to deliver talks on law, rights and perhaps even debate on theology - all before the age of 13. They would have learned the *Trivium* of logic, grammar and rhetoric. The strength of public speaking skill learned by these sons (daughters were of course excluded) of elites further supplemented their education by attending debating clubs, private religious sermons and fee-paying schools giving them advantages unimaginable to their less-privileged working-class peers who were either devoid of an education entirely or only taught the most subservient manners of *The Word*. Even today, looking across the vast vista of social inequality little has changed.

For explaining this I will use a little personal experience which all too well illustrates the enormous gap between the common man and the elite.

In my first foray at a university education, I was lucky enough to be accepted to the *School of Oriental and African Studies* (SOAS) in London. I was to live an hour's tube-ride away in a stereotypical terraced house alongside five other students in a particularly dingy room. Paying £644 in rent month and living on only £15 a week for food consisting of mostly eggs, tinned fish (which coincidentally resembled my travel to and from the School) and free vegetarian curry from the local Hare Krishna temple, I rapidly dropped from 70kg (154lbs) to 55kg (121lbs) in less than two years – a little underweight for someone 185cm (6') tall.

At this university I was enrolled to study the Japanese language and East Asian Sociology. In my view, there is no place outside of Japan which holds higher prestige than perhaps *Oxford* or *Cambridge* (by name alone) to learn this beautiful, if infuriatingly complex language. Its hallowed halls had been trod by Princes, Princesses, Emperors, Dictators, occasionally MI5 and the UK police's special branch with more than one students being supposedly frogmarched from the building after advocating for some less than conformist political viewpoints. A typical British understatement would be the claim that it was an *interesting* place to study at. Yet, it was the library where I would reside. For it was there I could escape from the abject cruelty that was a true British class-divide.

For my international readers who are lucky enough to have not experienced a class divide, it is quite difficult to describe. Class division is not as cruel as racism or the caste system, because people are judged not on the colour of their skin but the sound of their voice and the weight of their parent's wallet. The English elite often own hundreds if not thousands of acres of land or entire cities granted to their forefathers for services rendered to the crown almost a thousand years ago. Little much but attendance to state banquets has been offered since – the property was certainly not earned. Unlike in America where it is possible to own a few acres, in England this is the domain purely of those with generational wealth whose children's, children's, children and their children, will never have need to work a day of their life. Imagine then studying alongside the offspring of these elite.

Studying together with these students was either enlightening or demoralising. I remember a daughter of a well-known socialite asking me what my life was like working down a coal mine as a 'lamplight' (a child-labour occupation which was made illegal in 1842) before I came to university. Another, the son of a Lord, was perplexed that a debit card was capable of running out of money - "*surely it resets each day, no?*". The son of a political family would regularly badger me with the question "*...is it true you had to buy all your own furniture?*" and "*...why do you all choose to live in such tiny little houses?*" seemingly unaware that 16-bedroom stately homes passed from generation to generation were not something everyone was lucky enough to own.

Having a broad Yorkshire accent (which to my international readers is best regarded as a farmer's tongue) and being unable to 'go for drinks' (read: attend the invitation only gentleman's clubs at £120 per meal) left me open to ridicule by a number of my classmates. Being branded 'a product of ill-breeding from up-North' (a supposedly working-class area of England) was also part and parcel of studying alongside these so-called elite. Once again, the language used was telling of how these people thought of themselves and others. I'd almost say the experience outside of the library and classroom was unenjoyable.

One would hope those which society brands as 'elite' would practice morality and virtue. Sadly, this was often not the case and these prejudices were no-doubt ideals learned at home, propagated by parents with antiquated ideals of divine right to rule and worsened only by vile 'poverty pornography' television programs which flourished under the Conservative government, aimed at demonising the unemployed, the disabled or the unwell.

Now this is not to say all these sons and daughters were obnoxious or out of touch. I am certain a number of my classmates were phenomenally wealthy in their own regard but still acted with grace and humility. Yet, what was most striking was the difference between similar working-class students such as myself and the children of these elite when tasked with talking in public. Forgoing the middle-class who seemed to either flounder between mediocre or be bombastically over-confident, the prodigies of these echelons of society were usually a world amongst themselves thanks to years of elite schooling granting them confidence in their oratorical skill. A student taught in their primary years to recite poetry praising the digging for potatoes, the joys of being dustbin men and the delights to be found hunting for rats in wartime trenches will have a strikingly weakened lexicon compared to one wise in the ways of Chaucer, Byron and Rudyard Kipling.

You may be wondering why then have the common people not been privy to such a valuable education? Why would a government disempower its people so? Surely it doesn't cost more to teach these skills?

There are numerous theories explaining the dearth of such training from the sensible to conspiratorial and although this is not a work on political theory, nor a diatribe on societal influence, I believe it to be quite obvious. *Control.*

In the 1860's the British Government, yielding to the pressure of an education-demanding public began establishing a schooling system which was supposedly to benefit all of society. Schools were to be made available to the masses, rather than solely the upper classes. It was at this crucial juncture that the government of the time, led by the Liberal (in the Victorian sense of the word) *Prime Minister Lord John Russell,* had the opportunity to establish an equal system which would serve to elevate all, regardless of class or creed. However, with such a grand opportunity available to enrich the people, the government only inflamed class differences with the establishment of education commissions, whose recommendations entrenched vastly differing subjects to be taught to further enforce societal control. Rather than providing society with an equally well-educated populous, children from the working class would be expected to learn theology by rote and little else. One critic of the system would claim:

· · ·

"The child who leaves school at the age of fourteen will have attended some 2,000 or 3,000 reading lessons in the course of his school life. From these, in far too many cases, he will have carried nothing away but the ability to stumble with tolerable correctness through printed matter of moderate difficulty. He will not have carried away from them either the power or the desire to read".[1]

For the working class it was an emphasis on ideal handwriting which was praised, rather than composition of words and thought. Errors in cursive script written on slate blackboards were met with a severe caning. In comparison, the middle class would be treated to knowledge of mathematics, geography and literature, whereas the elite would learn the all-encompassing liberal *Trivium* which crucially included the studies of philosophy, rhetoric and grammar. Linguistic power was being funnelled upwards out of fear of an educated working class.[2]

In my view, it still is. The UK government still propagates what is known as a 'post code lottery' where living at the opposite side of a well-to-do street has the potential to relegate a child to an underfunded school which has failed inspections. Boundaries are regularly re-drawn to ensure the families of wealthy children are able to attend similarly fabulously wealthy institutions.

Across the pond, the United States of America in its comparatively short history has faced similar challenges. Despite establishing early schools in the 1830's, mandatory education was not passed through legislature until 1917, with debates on the benefits of educating raging as late as 1972 among Amish communities.[3] In 2011, a particularly regressive GOP repealed critical thinking skills-centric education in Texas stating "*...we oppose the teaching of higher order thinking skills,* *critical thinking skills and similar programs...[which] have the purpose of challenging the student's fixed beliefs and undermining parental authority*".[4] Such draconian measures may explain a large number of today's societal woes amongst some in America's society. A generation who have been taught that critical thought is dangerous is nothing more than fodder for the meat grinder and labour for the exploitative employer. These are the people who will speak like mortals if they do not train themselves otherwise.

The sad reality is that if societies and governments taught even the basic contents of this book, its production would have been unnecessary. Confident communication, true thought-articulation and an understanding of rhetoric would be as common to all as a loaf of sliced bread.

RHETORIC: IT'S NOT JUST RHYME, RHYTHM AND REASON

He steps on stage and draws the sword of rhetoric, and when he is through, someone is lying wounded and thousands of others are either angry or consoled.

PETE HAMILL

Rhetoric. When reading that word what comes to mind? Perhaps you think of wartime propaganda which tells you 'united we win, divided we fall'. Perhaps it's the corporate public relations department which announces they are 'realigning resources to match our attenuated corporate strategy' rather than firing employees after some unionised and demanded better pay. Or perhaps it's the political soundbite which proudly declaims *'Veni vidi vici* - I came, I saw, I conquered'.

These are all examples of the use of rhetoric, but not specifically rhetoric itself. Rhetoric is the modulation of language to bypass critical thought and appeal to our base emotions. It's the claim that nine out of ten doctors recommend a branded toothpaste (never mind that the tenth was a quack), it's the rhyme and rhythm in the slogan of your favourite cereal (snap, crackle and pop), it's the nationalistic jingo which dehumanises immigrants and minorities (that ghetto is a disgusting rat and rodent infested mess).

When you read the word 'rhetoric', perhaps it's a good idea to bundle the word with 'persuasion', because it contains a bit of everything persuasive. The concepts of loud and clear speech, logic, or even threatening someone with a gun are all rhetorical - if your victim capitulates to you and hands over their trinkets, you've probably persuaded them to do so with a word or two. There's a reason highwaymen adopted the phrase '*your money or your life*'; although those who heard it were most likely paying more attention to the barrel end of a gun than the repetitive *anaphora*.

Instead of offering techniques on how to best become a freebooter, purloiner or embezzler, this section will focus on a brief history of rhetoric and a small number of examples which will benefit your thought-articulation practice.

The origins of rhetoric are debated. They can currently be traced back to ancient Sumerian Cuneiform ideal poetic structural rules written by the Priestess *Enheduanna* of the Akkadian Empire during 2285 – 2250 B.C.[1]

Ancient Egyptians later considered 'wise silence' to be the grandest of all rhetorical devices as it was seen as one which was more persuasive than any turn of phrase.[2]

In Ancient Athenian times, the master Greek orators were *Pericles* (495 – 429 B.C.) and *Demosthenes* (384 – 322 B.C.)

SPEAK YOUR WAY TO WEALTH

who both added to what we consider to be our *rhetorical cannon* – a set of standardised best practices to persuade any audience, namely *Ethos*, *Logos* and *Pathos*. Pericles was a highly influential individual in Greek political society born from a wealthy background. During his youth, he was privy to all manner of lessons concerning public speaking and was described to have 'carried the might of Zeus with his words' with an uncanny ability to strike as lightning at his subject with an often-arrogant air. Demosthenes on the other hand was an orphan child born with a severe stutter and raised in poverty. After being deprived of his father's sword-making factory he was fabled to have recited poems and verse whilst running to improve his lung capacity, along with speaking with pebbles in his mouth to bolster his enunciation in hopes to convince a jury of his inheritance rights. He would succeed and would be initially hired as a speech writer, later becoming a master of rhetoric and political debate. However, he was not a true extemporaneous speaker and unlike Pericles his speeches were often highly passionate and appealed to the audience by ensuring to use layman terminology.

Ancient Rome would later adapt many of the rhetorical methods developed in Ancient Greece. The Romans saw oratorical and rhetorical skill as being a necessary part of personal development, with grand speeches often being delivered in the Senate where so much as a misplaced vowel sound could lead to hissing and boos from the capricious audience. *Marcus Tullius Cicero* (106 B.C. – 43 B.C.) a statesman, lawyer, scholar and Academic Skeptic would soon pen *Orator*, a text on the ideals of persuasive language stressing the importance of discovering one's personal style. However, his empire was not to last and with the fall of ancient Rome and the introduction of *Pleaders* (individuals who were paid handsomely to applaud poor speeches) oratorical skill would wane with *Pliny the Elder* (23 – 79 A.D.), a friend of Emperor *Vespasian* (9 – 24 A.D.), leaving the world with the words *'...you may rest assured that he who is the worst speaker has the loudest applause'.*[3]

Throughout East Asia, there was also little in the way of rhetorical skill practiced outside of poetry. *Confucius* (551 – 479 B.C.) saw efforts of linguistic persuasion outside talking *'righteously, cautiously, reflectively, and slowly'* as being an act of moral failure - silence and silence alone should shame one into submission.[4] It could be said such ideals are still enforced in the modern age through the Chinese Communist Party and its draconian means of control. In comparison, during the Heian Period (794-1185 A.D.), Japan differed from the Western style via the so-called *'tempura rhetoric.'* This rhetoric, much like the delicious batter which obscures the food beneath, expected one to give examples, facts and support for their argument in such a way that the listener would not even be aware an argument was being made until the closing statement was delivered – rather appropriate for a culture which eschews confrontation in favour of consensus. Korean rhetoric, which enshrined the notion of sharing one's emotions in a circumlocutionary manner to avoid causing offense – making reading between the lines a mandatory requirement differed also.

Rhetoric has to be found in religion also. In comparison to Christian sermons which were laden with repetitive denouncements of suffering, Asian courts tended to focus on the private recitals of droning Buddhist sutras rather than warnings of fire and brimstone to the trembling populace. In general, public speaking was (and in some instances still does) remains to be especially limited in Asia due to the restrictions levied upon the once merchant and farmer classes. With little being recorded in the way of ideal styles aside honorifics, linguistic formalities and executions for non-adherence it may be that individuals were praised for their voices at the time, but what exists has been lost to history.

Looking back to the West, the Middle ages and Renaissance periods led to a general decline in the importance of rhetoric and public speaking due to widespread illiteracy; the art was now mainly confined to the educated clergy and their weekly sermons. If written rhetoric was used, it was most likely that nailed to a church door by Lutheran-types. Alas, town criers and visiting Knights were still a necessity to declaim the Word of God through the demands of Kings and Queens, but little was allowed in the way of rhetorical flourish by these speakers - under pain of death.

Later in 1300 A.D., the largest European library was the university library of Paris, which had only 300 handwritten manuscripts. The usual cost of purchasing a book being that of a large house. No doubt they contained a plethora of rhetorical techniques. Yet, few could read, thus exceptions were allowed for paid readers and musicians who would visit taverns to recount war stories, local news or scandals using a mixture of rhetorical devices in their storytelling. Yet, even with the invention of the Guttenberg press which one hoped would lead to a boon in rhetoric, historian *Ada Palmer* quite bluntly quipped: *"...congratulations, you've printed 200 copies of the Bible; there are about three people in your town who can read the Bible in Latin, what are you going to do with the other 197 copies?"*.[5]

English language rhetoric would only experience a significant re-emergence with the works of *Shakespeare* (1564 – 1616 A.D.), with The Bard penning some of the most memorable rhetoric in history with the line *"Why, I can smile and murder whiles I smile"* in *Richard III.*

It would only be with the later founding of what would be called the *Elocutionist Movement* in the 18th century alongside the establishment of governments in England, France and America which led to a renewed need for public speakers. Empowered citizens, no longer serfs at the mercy of feudal rulers now instead had governments, chambers of office and guilds each with a voice demanding to be heard. This longing to articulate generationally suppressed needs would mobilise millions to the study of ideal facial expressions, gesture, posture and movement when speaking. Similarly, Victorian society became obsessed with beauty, eloquence and dignity in all its forms. Society would soon be flooded with texts and schooling on the topic summoning a new golden age. Much as I remember the nostalgia of the Pokémon craze during my childhood, should you have been born in the 18th century (and have been lucky enough to read and write) you may have spent your time composing sonnets with similar zeal. If a child were fortunate enough to be afforded an education on the topic, they would have been subject to schooling which would have put a modern literary degree to shame.

However, the *Elocutionists Movement* talked themselves into a corner. Universities began to see rhetorical studies as being capable of merely empowering Sophists who could artfully mask their ignorance rather than demand change. With the coming of the Edwardian 19th century, Imperialists and Industrialists demanded obedient soldiers and unquestioning workers, rather than individualistic souls capable of standing on a soap-box making rallying cries for unionization, meritocracy or peace. Such abilities were only to be granted to the elite. The public schooling system was to train efficient factory labourers, ranks gathered from among the working class; meanwhile the likes of the private schools of *Harrow, Eton, Oxford*, and *Cambridge* awaited the echelons who supposedly had ordained use for linguistic prowess.

In the 1950's *Field Marshal Bernard Montgomery* would reference how this funnelling of education impacted those who fought and died in the Great Wars:

"The soldiers of the second war were totally different people to those of the first war, because they were educated. In the first war the best recruiting Sargent was 'starvation' - off the streets! You didn't enlist in the army unless you were starving. So naturally you see, they went out into the first war and they did what they were told, and the Generalship, I always think of the first war, would not have done in this second war with these highly educated people who could think and appreciate and wanted to know what was going on."

Perhaps 'Monty' was predicting how the United Kingdom of Great Britain would, as it currently is, experience a pernicious demonisation of education to return people back to an unthinking state - only able to follow orders given to them by their supposed superiors.

Arguably however, it was the 'fireside chats' of *Franklin D. Roosevelt* which led to the ultimate waning of the oratorical-rhetorical style. Despite the reverence for Lincoln and his liberating words, citizens began to demand less in the way of grand speeches with poetic aphorism and instead longed for more informal conversations. Millions had grown tired of being spoken at and instead wished to be spoken with. Now this is not to say FDR was a poor speaker, he was a rhetorical genius in his own right. Even *Winston Churchill*, a man who was later universally praised for his own rhetorical methodologies of raising the morale of the public, could not motivate the English people to sustain his leadership after the victory of war had understandably left their interests elsewhere. After World War II, many began to see rhetoric as the language of the propagandist and the oppressor, with oratorical skill later being seen in the same light as mass-manipulation given *Adolph Hitler's* atrocious displays on stage.

Learning this, you may then assume rhetoric is a dangerous blight upon our language, but this is not so. Without rhetoric, society would most likely stagnate. There would be no revolutions to free the enslaved. No movements to demand political reform. No Shakespeare to write *"...the first thing we do, let's kill all the lawyers"* in Henry VI. You will have used rhetoric at some point without realising it. You may have uttered something which convinced another to your point of view, you may have repeated a well-known phrase to aid with explanation or composed a poem which rhymed. These are all rhetorical techniques.

No occupation excludes the rhetorician. *Elihu Burritt* (1810 – 1879) also known as *the learned blacksmith* due to his boyhood spent reading books during his sixteen-hour workday at the forge, was considered a master of the written and spoken word. Writing on the misuse of rhetoric he said:

"Those orators who give us much noise and many words, but little argument and less wit, and who are the loudest when least lucid, should take a lesson from the great volume of nature; she

often gives us the lighting without the thunder, but never the thunder without the lighting."[6]

Yet, like everything in this world, it can be used for good and evil. Both *Winston Churchill* and *Adolf Hitler* used rhetoric; one for good and the other for evil. Repetition rhetoric was used when *Winston Churchill* so valiantly declaimed *"...We shall fight on the beaches, we shall fight on the landing grounds, we shall fight in the fields and in the streets, we shall fight in the hills; we shall never surrender..."* and *Adolf Hitler* used the same technique when he propagated the Führer-myth of leadership supremacy with the similarly repetitive *"...Ein Volk, Ein Reich, Ein Führer* (One People, One Nation, One Leader)".

If not for rhetoric, every mind would have to be won by logic and logic alone. Without rhetoric there would be no groupthink, no societies, nor common proscriptions. Each individual with their untold variations of needs, wants and unique thoughts would have to be convinced by logical argument. *Spock* from *Star Trek* thought in pure logic and look at the trouble that got him into.

What then if you wish to learn to use and identify rhetoric? One of the easiest ways of learning rhetoric is to note down phrases which you find to be pleasant to read or impactful on the ear and examine exactly why they appeal to you – just as you would when trying to figure out which herbs and spices work well with others and which concoctions leave a foul taste in the mouth. Do these pleasing phrases rhyme, perhaps each word starts with the same letter, is there a poetic element, or does it utilise three repetitions of the same word? Much as all great writers have found; there is no shame to be found in repeating the words of others – so long as you improve them.

Here are three easy to learn rhetorical devices you can include with your thought-articulation practice:

Anaphora:

Anaphora is quite simple, it's the repetition of a phrase. A fine example is shown here taken from *Charles Dickens'* (1859) *A Tale of Two Cities*:

"It was the best of times, it was the worst of times, it was the age of wisdom, it was the age of foolishness, it was the epoch of belief, it was the epoch of incredulity, it was the season of light, it was the season of darkness, it was the spring of hope, it was the winter of despair."

Anadiplosis:

Anadiplosis is when a speaker or writer ends and begins a phrase with the same words such as the chain of events speech in *Richard II* by *William Shakespeare*:

"The love of wicked men converts to fear; that fear to hate, and hate turns one or both; to worthy danger and deserved death."

In *Star Wars, Episode 1: The Phantom Menace*, Yoda used anadiplosis: *"Fear is the path to the dark side; fear leads to anger; anger leads to hate; hate leads to suffering."*

Tricolon:

A tricolon is a sentence made of three words or consisting of three short phrases and is sometimes referred to as 'the rule of three'. Tricolon's are effective, because the brain loves to find patterns.

English pubs are usually named with a tricolon with establishments such as *The Bulls Head, Rose and Crown* and *Duke of York*.

The Great and Powerful Oz used a tricolon when he proudly declaimed *"...You are talking to a man who has laughed in the face of death, sneered at doom, and chuckled at catastrophe!"*

One more example of using a tricolon effectively is to build the emotion steadily, much like the difference between those initial heavy breaths one takes when climbing a mountain and the euphoria one feels when summiting the peak.

Learning the vast cannon of rhetoric is a noble goal, but is beyond the scope of this book. Should you wish to learn more there are numerous magnificent works on the topic and perhaps the most notable is *Mark Forsyth's* (2013) *The Elements of Eloquence: How to Turn the Perfect English Phrase*.

WHAT DO YOU REALLY THINK?

I believe, that I shall never be old enough to speak without embarrassment when I have nothing to say.

ABRAHAM LINCOLN

Some people live within a prison of their own experiences. Others are subservient only to the values of others. Both rarely say what they truly think.

When explaining how emotion or ingrained conditioning can masquerade how we truly feel, I often ask my students to outline a minor ideal they believe to be part of their nature and explain why. This often results with a quote, a buzzword or an opinion which has been repeated ad-infinitum by their peers rather than one subjected to critical thought or Socratic questioning.

Explaining how these repetitions are not a true explanation of their ideals, I am usually met with an awkward silence and a sudden realization that the ideals, values or opinions held have been followed blindly without introspection. Some take it well, others don't.

Attempting to articulate these previously uninspected thoughts can often result in a blank stare and a grasping for words, as if they were desperately attempting to grab the banks of a shore before drowning. Despite how embarrassing this may be at first, it is one of the great illuminators to the timeless adage of '*Know Thyself*' which is impossible without practicing thought-articulation.

Yet, there are those who know neither themselves nor anything of the topic at hand, who can still speak and make much noise but say very little. This apparent 'gift of the gab' often develops in those who have been taught that the lack of an opinion is shameful.

In my view, it is the sign of an honourable person to withhold judgement on topics they have not carefully considered rather than to speak something uninformed. Yet, in today's world, being ignorant of the latest hype, political scandal or celebrity sensation is seen as an unpardonable travesty by some. Online, the world demands people hold a particular viewpoint, that they offer comment on how they feel or virtue signal. Often an opinion is demanded by anyone in the name of providing 'balance'. Yet we have gone too far. The scales have been tipped. Capitulating to this demand we see on national television flat-earth conspiracists aside geographers, spiritualists aside scientists and homeopathists aside doctors. Providing balance has allowed in some circles the nonsense of Holocaust-denial and Cultural Marxism to become acceptable choices for debate which only a decade prior would have been a harrowing notion to even consider.

When listening to the ignorant who are called upon to provide balance, you can eventually see how skewed viewpoints have mired their opinions, how they squirm under scrutiny and how they often resort to repeating fallacies or *ad hominem* attacks in effort to protect the fragility of their ego. Truth is usually accompanied by clarity, humility, and even a plain earnestness of style. "Truths" that depend upon parroting and parlour tricks are usually masquerading lies.

Although the pendulum of balance has swung out of step for the moment, I hope for the days when experts and experts alone return to the fore. Yet, the damage has been done and millions have fallen under the spell of repeating ill-formed ideas and fallacies in thought and voice. Why?

Sociologists say we accept ideas we don't understand to foster a sense of tribal belonging, but I don't think that's the whole story. A quirk of human nature is that our brain subconsciously remembers many, perhaps even all of our experiences. While some memories may be vibrant and others obscured, each experience added to our memory by our thought engraver is influential. Saving memories both relevant and irrelevant often causes us to harbour subconscious biases that lie latent until the opportunity arrives to revisit them once more. We soon find our mental 'blank slate' is more a mottled canvas, painted over so many times that we aren't always sure what lies beneath. This isn't always detrimental of course; biases, prejudices, suspicions and hunches often serve as a shortcut, where we would otherwise be exhausted by repetitive mental journeys. Biases can save our wallets from scams, protect our bodies from harm or keep our minds free from vice. Yet, if left unchecked, this uncontested handing down of unfair judgment can become insidious. It can ruin personalities, destroy opportunities or even lead to illness and death.

What then is one to do? My advice is again to examine your opinions aloud. To extemporise upon them whenever possible.

In my view, there are two forms of opinions. Those sound and those unsound. The sound opinion has been subject to critical thought, introspection, the ridding of prejudice and a letting-go of preconceived ideas. It need not have withstood the rigours of peer-review, but it should have been exposed to the various elements of debate, even if only by solitary verbalised internal-dialogue, rather than kept within a protective vacuum or echo chamber. Sound opinions are often easily articulated, because they have been scrutinised and tested.

In comparison, an unsound opinion is based on emotional reaction, uninspected prejudices, opposition to change and insidious lazy thinking. Unsound opinions range from the innocuous - a child refusing to eat their vegetables due to a past dislike - all the way up to the malevolent - hatred of those we have never truly known for qualities we have been programmed to dislike; megalomaniacal political schemes to force one's will upon an unwilling world, and even denial of facts as though reality is subject to pick-and-choose curation. Each instance is united by the same temper-tantrum - a flat refusal to engage with whatever one feels resentful towards.

To cultivate a sound opinion however is often not an easy task. Yet, it is a necessary one to aid with clear articulation of your thoughts.

Sadly, the world presents three major barriers which hinder the unbiased thinker:

- First, prejudices which arise from our emotions, environment and peers.

- Second, prejudices which arise from a lack of critical introspection.

- Third, prejudices which arise from false testimony by malicious actors.

An understanding of how each impacts the way we feel about a topic will aid towards establishing a sound opinion made of rational thought.

Vaccination is an excellent example to consider when discussing how prejudices form; for the reality is that vaccines are unequivocally safe and necessary for the survival of the human race. For those who wish for a world without vaccines, they need only observe the world under the threat of Covid-19 with its millions of preventable deaths to see a world without *one*.

Vaccines have eliminated some of the most vile diseases to afflict mankind. They have destroyed smallpox, banished Ebola and consigned Polio's cruel iron lung to the museum. Yet, despite all this good, anti-vaccine conspiracists prevail. Once eradicated diseases, have returned to blight our kind due to the influence of the uninformed and the crook. Rationality and reason has been usurped by hysteria and absurdity. Research is considered by some to be merely the viewing of memes, blog posts or spurious videos which align with their worldview rather than critique and earnest discussion. Their minds are closed tight like those under the spell of a cultish religion.

But why do some fall afoul of such a closed mind? The world has seen how recently, millions who spent their time mingling with the minds of ill-formed opinions have been seduced by predominantly right-wing narratives claiming vaccines to be the Devil's work or a plot for microchipping. In despair these lonely people are twisted by lies and propaganda, turning once accepting types into super spreader neurotics. These people often merely form snap judgements and ill-considered sentiments based on misunderstandings of jargon – they have undertaken little in the way of critical introspection. When asked to explain their views, they stumble, falter, struggle and frequently leave the listener with either a blank stare or a denial to comment on the matter - lest it shatter their ego.

Here then are three reasons suggesting how you can avoid holding such unsound opinions.

Using Covid-19 as a supporting example, there may be those who early on in their life experienced the sharp prick of a misplaced injection during their inoculations leading them to be scared of needles. This memory of pain may have long faded, yet the subconscious still remains wary of the offending implement. A dread of the doctor follows, perhaps the individual then learns of some freak accident at a hospital or a one in a million side-effect strikes them as 'common'. In an effort to entrench the dangers of vaccines, the ego seeks for information which validates its fear. Taking to the internet, the trembling reader then finds similarly uninformed, like-minded peers who validate their judgements with tales of woe, horror and despair. Surrounded in this echo chamber, the unvaccinated now falls under the spell of ignorance and sadly, is most likely the first to die from or pass on a disease of which exists a vaccine. Only the escape from this echo chamber will bring about fresh ideas, understanding and a new conviction in their mind.

On the other hand, there may be those who have no innate fear of needles. Perhaps they regularly visit their doctor. Yet, through a failing of education or a lackadaisical approach to critical introspection, they are left with a limited knowledge of basic medical science. They may be curious as to the contents of a vaccine and stumble across some honest material outlining how an active component is 'genetic material'. These two words then trigger an ill-informed and preconceived advertising slogan which suggests genetically modified food is 'unsafe'. The notion that such material will warp their body into something unnatural then establishes itself and the uninformed opinion begins to solidify. Of course, critical introspection shows that each item we eat contains some form of genetic material in the way of cells and DNA. The human body cannot survive on water alone. Genetically modified food is necessary for the survival of the human race and it is no different than selective cross-pollination. One need only observe the difference between a non-genetically modified banana and a modified one to see the amount of consumable flesh has increased almost tenfold. Should one be informed of this basic medical fact and rationality preserve, they should have no concern with a vaccine. It was the acceptance of the facts which set them free. That is, unless their knowledge of the 'facts' has been tainted by the malicious actor who masquerades the vile as virtuous.

Most pitiful of all is the opinion formed by the intentional giving of false testimony. Malicious actors are perhaps one of the great dangers of our age. 'Doctors' who break the Hippocratic oath for profit with their treacherous, odious and baseless claims have been responsible for the deaths of millions of poor uninformed souls, whose minds were warped after they sought only stability and hope. Opinions parroted by these victims are often the words of charlatans, quacks and frauds who in their grand-titled books, stories or pamphlets plagued with scaremongering pages promise reformation of the real. These are the *deepfakes*; the claims that vaccines are dangerous; that all is not as it seems; and they and they alone hold the answer to some great conspiratorial secret. In reality, these are nothing more than deceptive ploys aimed to seduce and manipulate. Line after line of immoral rhetoric, their messianic claims, lies and manipulation of honest statistics aim to twist the judgements of the innocent, to undermine the rationality of their thought and to goad them to parrot their prophetic words rather than inspect their claims. Lacking any depth, these works play on innate fears, misunderstandings and fallacies. They do nothing but harm. Such conmen deserve only to be defrocked, ridiculed and punished in hopes that they repent, renounce their words and change their ways before millions more die at their hands.

Therefore, to avoid falling for these fallacies ask yourself:

- Are there opinions in your mind which have been unduly influenced by your environment, emotions or peers?

- Are some malformed due to a lack of understanding?

- Are there others which are twisted by the malicious actor, who aimed only to scare and seduce you in search of profit?

All of these fallacies can be identified through rigorous thought-articulation.

Before forming a strong opinion, you must first example the impartiality of your thoughts. If you feel strongly towards something, such as a hatred of a particular ideology, yet you are unable to define exactly why, it is most probable you only believe so due to an external force or mantra which has usurped your critical thinking and internal-dialogue. 'Blind prejudice' is aptly named, because it causes one to become blind to the truth.

Begin then to articulate your opinion. Say your thoughts aloud and attempt to explain exactly *why* you feel the way you do. Attempt to justify your emotions through logic. Question if you have proof for the claims made. Examine any weaknesses that arrive and delve deep into the gaps of your knowledge by earnest study of information which has been subject to peer-review.

In examining your opinions, you will no-doubt soon find how a broad range of your preconceived ideas, thoughts and ideologies could be ill-informed or may have been accumulated without proper verification or introspection. This is nothing to be ashamed of. Rather than engaging in self-sabotage and hate who you once were, be grateful you have found the malleability of mind to change how you think and feel.

On the other hand, should you find your opinions confirmed via cross-examination of evidence, be similarly humble that you came across information which was true, rather than malicious.

The thinker of today finally faces a problem brand-new to our species - an overabundance of information. Historically, ignorance for want of information had been our sole ill. Yet now, ignorance due to an utter excess of information is arguably an even greater threat. When confronted with the limitless, ungovernable contents of the internet, two damaging temptations emerge: either to select the dogmatic worldview that most appeals to one's ego, or to give up on the intellectual pursuit entirely, like one who starves at a feast due to an inability to choose where to begin.

In both cases, a middle-ground of moderation is the solution – you must begin with and then master the basics. While all others bicker over cursory minutia, having the self-respect to go back to the beginnings of those subjects you find most meaningful and work your way up from there will serve you well. It is better to know a little, and know it well, than to be an inch deep and a mile wide. Those who have the discipline to do things the old-fashioned way, to study, struggle and discern, are about to be afforded the ultimate chance to distinguish themselves from those who are doomed to mimic the mob.

In a time when most conventional vocations are to be automated and most stores of information are becoming hopelessly undermined, it is the critical thinkers and articulate free speakers who will be rendered the essential workers, for their merits shall allow them to speak their way to wealth.

CHAPTER 4

THOUGHT-ARTICULATION STRUCTURES

It usually takes me more than three weeks to prepare a good impromptu speech.

MARK TWAIN

In this chapter, you will learn an adaptable structure to help articulate your thoughts and say what you think to either yourself or others. The keyword is *adaptable*.

In some instances, you need not provide a visual description of the topic, in others you need not propose a question. However, by following this structure during your private practice sessions it will allow for you to cover a wider gamut of thought-articulation.

- Define the topic.

- Provide a visual description.

- Add a metaphor.

- Give an interesting fact or point.

- Propose and answer a question.

- End with a Gordian knot.

The practice of avoiding mindless speech, the act of earnest thought inspection and the giving of two-minute extemporaneous talks using this thought-articulation structure has been the maker of hundreds of my clients. Its ability to transform your speaking abilities cannot be overestimated. It takes only two minutes to practice, yet its results may last a lifetime.

WHAT EXACTLY ARE WE TALKING ABOUT?

Clear thought makes clear speech.

To begin with, you should always avoid engaging in *duportism* when speaking. Should you *duport* at any time during your speech, you will only make a fool of yourself. However, as this is quite obvious I shall make no further mention of the act.

Reading the above statement probably didn't make sense. You may have furrowed your brow in annoyance, or perhaps your mind began to wander elsewhere. Don't worry; both 'duport' and 'duportism' are not real words, they were nonsensical terms which I created to prove a point - that much as a cook cannot create a delicious meal without first deciding which ingredients to use, a speaker cannot talk extemporaneously or articulate their thoughts clearly without being able to define the words they speak.

Being able to define something equals true understanding, but lacking an understanding of word definitions is a major stumbling block towards clear, coherent and concise thought-articulation. Now, this isn't to say you need to go and purchase an etymologic dictionary. Instead, you only need to question if the word you are using best defines your thoughts, because a clearly stated point is better than an hour's confused thinking.

Many people struggle to make their point clearly because they have not defined exactly what they are talking about. This is often the case when two people are involved in an argument; days, months and years may go by with little change, only for the two to realise they were arguing about different things. No amount of debate would have solved the issue unless they had first defined the problem at hand.

How then do you achieve strong definition skills? When I struggle with a concept, it is usually because I am unable to break its key factors down into simplistic parts and translate those elements into my own words. I frequently work with university students who struggle with the same issue who resort to carelessly repeating misunderstood quotes, leading to ridicule. This is also the case for those in the corporate world. Despite seemingly understanding the content of meetings, staff are often unable to translate this emotional understanding onto paper or articulate it to their peers. Poorly organised corporate training leads to similar issues. The reason for both problems is almost always the same; it is neither a matter of poor revision technique nor intellectual inadequacy, but a failing to create a personal definition of specialist terminology.

For example; the word 'synergy' may appeal to the C-suite, but if junior employees are unaware its true meaning is 'team work' such a buzzword is of little use in the mind of those who are told to practice it. This lack of understanding of concepts leads to individuals of all ages being unable to translate crucial information into their own words; ultimately stunting their future potential and leaving them feeling as if they are an intellectual failure.

Thankfully, all this can be overcome by ensuring to define any terminology which is not part of your everyday lexicon. By developing a wider understanding of your mother tongue (rather than merely a larger vocabulary), your enhanced linguistic abilities will also result in more eloquent thought-translation skill. Put differently, the more masterful one is of their first language, the more clear their very thinking will become. This resulting depth of examination allows for you to bring more material ideas from the subconscious into everyday speech, ultimately leading to increased confidence.

You can cultivate your definition skills by ensuring:

- Your definition can articulate the essential attributes of whatever is at hand.

- Your definition does not name the thing or concept being defined. For example: saying '*a circle is circular*' adds nothing of clarity. It would be better to say '*a circle is an infinitely looping object lacking straight lines*'.

- Your definition is neither too wide or narrow in its scope. It must be accessible to both yourself and a wider group of people.

- Your definition does not fall afoul of bias by using

language such as: '*the immoral are those who are not moral*'.

Curiously, it is often the case people believe they understand a particular word, term or concept, but in reality, it only exists in their memory due to rote memorization rather than true understanding. Being unable to define something is therefore akin to a 'verbal blind spot'. Failure to formulate a clear definition for these verbal blind spots will continue to hinder progress in its respective area. Perhaps you have come across a word in this book or elsewhere which you recognise, yet if asked to define it, your mind would draw a blank. These verbal blind spots can exist within their hundreds even among my most successful clients.

Thankfully again the solution to verbal blind spots is extremely simple: attempt to describe the offending error in your own words following the previous recommendations. On occasion this may involve consulting a dictionary, but with more concrete definitions at your disposal, your developing abilities will naturally lend credence to how you think and speak. This simple act will also prove particularly beneficial in improving your ability to read and study at a higher level.

However, a word of caution; you need not pepper each and every phrase with flowery definitions as this will seem overly explanatory, pompous and demeaning to the listener. Consult the following examples:

(*Disclaimer: in the following examples, I have chosen everyday objects rather than business jargon and terminology to be defined allowing the examples to be accessible to a wide range of readers. However, your practice is best performed by initially attempting* to first define random objects and then shifting your focus to defining terminology, phrases or subjects for discussion relating to your industry, hobby or studies. As defining your subject matter for discussion is the first step, a list of suitable subjects has been provided in at the end of this chapter should you need inspiration.)

Imagine the word 'stonemasonry' had been chosen at random for discussion. It is fair to assume being tasked to talk on this topic for two minutes may hinder many unless they are a stone mason. However, by first defining the word 'stonemasonry', it grants the speaker a strong foundation to build upon from their subconscious knowledge of the topic of stones, carving and statues among others.

Secondly, the words used when defining the topic will lead to a natural segue for expansion, 'incorporating a visual image' discussed in the next section.

The examples below are slightly-modified transcriptions from previous students, organised in their levels of linguistic complexity from simple to complex. Read the examples below and then attempt to define the topic yourself:

"The topic I have drawn is 'stonemasonry'. I must be honest and say I don't know much about it, but I do know that stonemasonry is when someone takes stone and carves it into different shapes for buildings and art."

"Stonemasonry is a challenging topic to talk about, but I am sure you are all well aware that the buildings which we walk into *each day did not spring up from the ground by themselves! Their parts once existed in varying shapes and sizes deep underground; probably at a quarry only a handful of miles away from where I'm stood. The shape of these bricks were formed by tools and nothing more."*

"Ladies and gentlemen, I stand here before you today to talk on the topic of 'stonemasonry'! Stonemasonry is the ancient art of taking rough, unhewn rock from the Earth and through repeated blows, chisels and careful refinement, shaping that once irregular and natural element into something ornate and beautiful. Stonemasonry involves the use of quarrymen, masons and carvers. Whilst not all rock is suitable for the mason, we can all benefit from their grand works. It is the removal of whatever stone surrounds the artists' imagination to chisel away until the angel inside is freed."

As you can see, even the first student who openly admitted they had little knowledge on the topic of *stonemasonry* managed to define the word, naturally causing them to segue onto the art of carving and shaping for the construction of buildings and art. Once the conscious mind had established the topic for discussion, the subconscious, in its wonderous ability to bring vast archives of memory to the fore, provided a suitable set of words for a strong definition.

In comparison, the second speaker provided a concrete outline of the topic, but at the time used a wide variety of gestures (pointing to the stone in the building he was stood in) to bolster his point to make up for a lack of knowledge on the topic.

However, the third speaker was especially effective in her definition, because she outlined what acts are involved in *stonemasonry* with an eloquent personal flair.

Let us try another example using the word; '*leaf*':

"A leaf is something which you can find on a tree. They come in lots of different shapes and sizes and their colour changes during the year from green to yellow-orange."

"Leaves are most magnificent things! In their short, one-year long lifespan these chlorophyll filled pockets are the bringers of life, the spreaders of O^2 and the dancers upon the wind. Why if it were not for that blessed, breathable air they bring us, I wouldn't even be here today!"

"Leaves are ephemeral and transitory. In Spring they hang high above our heads, in Summer they rustle alongside a cool breeze, in Autumn they crunch beneath our feet and in Winter they return to Mother Earth to act as mulch for a future harvest."

Notice how the first speaker explained that leaves came from trees, providing a simple yet effective description. Although struggling with poetic eloquence, their definition was ideal.

In comparison, the second speaker was seemingly struggling to define what leaves were and instead resorted to a poetic language rife with metaphor and scientific imagery, with no mention of trees; something quite obvious to outline. During this exercise he was especially nervous and effectively tried to make his words more majestic than they normally were. Despite being pleasant to listen to, the meaning may have been lost to some.

The third speaker assumed the audience knew the definition of the word 'leaf' and moved immediately onto similarly poetic language brimming with emotion, but in some instances, this would not have sufficed, especially if there where people from different climates listening. It would have therefore been better to use more simplistic language which better defined the topic.

Let us next choose a particularly nondescript and challenging topic; *'manhole covers'*:

"Manhole covers are not something I ever thought I'd be asked to talk about but here goes: they are brown or grey lids found above sewers and they are made from iron or plastic. That's about all I know."

"Manhole covers are the rectangular, brown, slabs of metal or stone that you see in the street above sewers or telecoms pipes. They have a raised crisscross pattern on them to stop you from slipping when you walk over them, they come in lots of different sizes and they usually have the name of the manufacturer on them."

"Manhole covers are protective coverings placed over sewage canals. Their design is functional but mundane and they often make an easily recognizable sound when driven over by a car. They come in varying shapes and sizes, usually round or

rectangular and are made from galvanized iron, composite plastics or concrete."

Can you identify the differences between the definitions of 'manhole covers'? Which do you think was the most effective and why?

Hopefully these examples have shown that poetic language is not a requirement for eloquent speaking, because if used ineffectively, it can become a barrier between yourself, your thoughts or any listening audience.

Yet, when embarking on this exercise you may initially be disappointed with your struggles. Much like writing, you must remember that the act of off-the-cuff composition is not a gift granted from birth – I have yet to hear a baby give a grand oration nor a client launch into this exercise without some hesitation. Skilful thought-articulation is an art which has to be learned and honed over years of repeated practice.

Thankfully, your training need not be as severe as the great orator *Demosthenes* (384 – 322 B.C.) who shaved half his head to ensure he stayed indoors practicing his language skills, kept a spear dangling above his shoulder to tame his gestures, only to then recite poetry whilst jogging with a mouthful of pebbles to improve his diction. Rather, your practice should be challenging but enjoyable with clearly defined goals in place. Aim to make one percent of improvement with each attempt. A simple unit of measurement could be the gradual removal of the verbal fillers *'umm'*, *'err'*, *'hmm'*, the increasing vividness of visual imageries used, the clarity of adjectives strung together or the impact of metaphors chosen.

The key takeaway from this chapter therefore is that before engaging in any thought-articulation practice, *you should be at least capable of defining the topic to be discussed.* In reality, it is notoriously difficult, if not impossible to speak on a topic you are unable to define and it is surprising how often you may have heard of a term, a phrase or a word but struggle to outline it.

WHAT DO YOU SEE?

Men are born with two eyes, but with one tongue, in order that they should see twice as much as they say.

CHARLES CALEB COLTON

After having first defined the topic, you should then incorporate a visual image to further bolster your ability to articulate your thoughts. All of the best-selling books have some form of visual imagery. This could be the description of the firing of guns in a historical recount, a vivid tale of demonic uprisings in a fantasy novel, or a medical dissection in a biology textbook.

For your practice in visual description, the language chosen should be brimming with adjectives and as gaudy as possible. You may want to imagine you are attempting to describe the object to someone over the telephone who has to draw a picture of it. You should engage in exaggeration for either comedic or serious effect – both will aid with your overall thought-articulation.

Some may wonder why describing an object is necessary, which is a valid question. The answer is simple; being able to translate your thoughts into pictures is an incredibly useful skill, because it appeals to the primal part of the human brain which still to this day loves storytelling.

Throughout history, all cultures have been found to rely upon storytelling to aid with learning and the passing on of important information. During our primitive days, mankind sat around a campfire describing the deathly dangers of wild beasts, the locations of food and safe spaces to find shelter, which may even have been accompanied by song or dance. You need not dance during your practice, but you can still use body language for great effect - of which will be discussed later.

Furthermore, second only to writing, attempting to describe the world around you in intricate speech often allows you to utter words and phrases often unintended or profound, which can often serve to aid with the expansion of your higher-level thinking.

Clear sight should thus be reflected with a clear description. Start by practicing to describe simple objects such as 2D shapes like squares, triangles and circles. Then shift to more complex 3D objects such as a toothbrush, a bottle and then items with moving parts. Finally, attempt to describe fiendishly difficult objects such as colours and liquids which will rely upon poetic descriptions rather than the literal. There is most likely a Nobel Prize in Literature awaiting anyone who can describe colour to those who are blind, so don't be disappointed if you can't achieve that one. The effort instead should be to simply practice.

I have found some students find this exercise difficult if they are predominantly logically minded, read little in the way of fictional material or have weak imaginational skills. Further still, if you are like myself and suffer from *aphantasia* (an inability to picture things in the mind's eye) this practice can be especially challenging. Given that, I have included a small list of suggested adjectives to aid with daily practice which can be supplemented with either one of the many lists available online or the wonderfully resourceful *Cassell Dictionary of Appropriate Adjectives* by E. K. Mikhail (1993). Yet, with a little practice, you can become quite adept at portraying the world around you in vibrant imagery.

Taking from this list of object shape adjectives, attempt to describe some items in your vicinity with these basic adjectives:

aerodynamic, angular, asymmetrical, bent, bulbous, chunky, clean, closed, concave, concentric, congruent, contorted, contoured, convex, convoluted, corrugated, cuboid, curly, curved, curvy, deformed, fitted, flat, forked, four-square, geometric, globular, graceful, malformed, misshapen,

oval, peaked, pointed, pointy, proportioned, regular, regularly, rolled-up, round, rounded, rugged, sculptured, shapely, silhouetted, sinuous, solid, square, straight, straight, sweeping, symmetrical, tapered, tapering, three-cornered, three-dimensional, twisted, two-dimensional, well-rounded, well-turned, wraparound

. . .

Now, using this list of colour-supporting adjectives attempt to describe the colour of your chosen object in more detail:

ablaze, bleached, bleak, blotchy, bold, brash, bright, brilliant, chintzy, clean, cold, colour-coded, colourful, cool, dappled, dark, deep, delicate, discoloured, dusty, electric, festive, fiery, flamboyant, flaming, fluorescent, fresh, glistening, glittering, glowing, harmonious, harsh, iridescent, loud, matching, mellow, multicoloured, opalescent, pastel, prismatic, psychedelic, pure, rich, sepia, showy, soft, sombre, splashy, tinged, tinted, two-tone, vibrant, vivid, warm, watery

Having now given the object at hand a clear description of its shape and colour, finally attempt to describe its features in further detail:

above, absorbing, absorptive, abstract, accidental, acoustic, acoustical, active, actual, addictive, additional, additive, adhesive, adjacent, adjoining, aerodynamic, aesthetic, algebraic, amazing, aromatic, atmospheric, atomic, attractive, average,

bactericidal, bad, base, basic, beneficial, binding, biological, biomechanical, bulk, caustic, cellular, characteristic, chemical, chief, cleansing, click, cognitive, cohesive, collective, commercial, common, complex, computational, conductive, constant, constitutive, contradictory, corresponding, corrosive, creative, critical, cultural, curative, curious,

. . .

dangerous, defined, definite, dependent, desirable, destructive, detailed, different, directional, distinctive, distinguishing, distressed, distributional, diverse, divine, drying, dynamic, ecclesiastical, elastic, electric, electrical, electronic, elementary, ending, energetic, enhanced, environmental, essential, exact, excellent, exceptional, exclusive, existing, expensive, explosive, extensive, external, extraordinary,

familiar, fattening, favourable, few, final, fine, first, fixed, fluid, fluorescent, following, font, foreign, formal, former, functional, fundamental, further, general, generic, genetic, geometric, geometrical, global, good, great, harmful, healing, healthful, hereditary, hidden, historic, human, hydraulic,

ideal, identical, important, improved, independent, individual, inducing, industrial, inherent, injurious, innate, intangible, intellectual, interesting, internal, intrinsic, irritating, key, kinetic, known, large, larger, largest, level, like, literary, little, local, logical,

macroscopic, magic, magical, magnetic, main, major, making, many, marvellous, material, mathematical, measurable, measured, mechanical, medical, medicinal, mental, mere, metallic, metric, metrical, microscopic, miraculous, molecular, moral, more, morphological, most, motivational, multiple, mysterious, mystic, mystical,

narcotic, natural, nearby, necessary, negative, neighbouring, new, nice, normal, nourishing, novel, numerical, numerous, nutritional, nutritious, objective, obvious, occult, old, older, only, opposite, optical, ordinary, organizational, original, other, outstanding, overall, owned,

particular, peculiar, perceptual, personal, pharmaceutical, phenomenal, physical, plastic, poisonous, positive, possible, potential, powerful, preservative, primary, principal, private, producing, projective, promising, promoting, protective, psychological, public, real, reflective, refractive, regenerative, regulatory, related, relational, relative, relevant, remarkable, rental, required, requisite, residential, resistant, respective, restorative, right, rural,

same, scale, secondary, select, semantic, sensible, sensitive, sensory, separate, several, shared, significant, similar, simple, singular, small, smaller, social, solvent, soothing, sound, spatial, special, specific, spectral, spiritual, stabilizing, standard, state, static, stimulating, strange, striking, structural, suitable, superior, supernatural, sustainable, symbolic,

tangible, technical, technological, text, theatrical, theoretical, therapeutic, thermal, toxic, true, typical, ultimate, underlying, undesirable, unexpected, uniform, unique, universal, unknown, unusual, upscale, urban, useful, usual, vacant, valuable, variable, various, vast, viscous, visible, visual, vital, wonderful

There are far more adjectives available for perusal in the aforementioned resources and this work is in no-way exhaustive. However, the information provided to you will serve as a suitable list for practice.

Much as a second language learner will initially struggle to describe even the most basic of thoughts, so too may you when attempting to describe an object or concept with the words you can recall in the moment. However, with every attempt comes increased fluency. Consult these examples of visual description written in the most basic style, to that employed by an art critic.

AN APPLE

"An apple is a round green fruit with a dimple on the top."

"The fruit called an apple is round and red or green on the outside, white and seeded on the inside, and grows on trees. It's quite shiny, but not to a mirror finish."

"An apple is a delectable fruit, whose external coloration ranges across the autumnal palette from greenish-yellow to blood-red. When picked and polished, its sheen may be especially reflective, and when sliced open, it reveals a fleshy pale pulp as tender as it is sweet. Ebony seeds capable of reproducing the entire fruit tree are nestled within its spiny structural core. A little stem juts out from the top of this core, and suspends the fruit from its tree branch like a gravitational apostrophe."

A PENCIL

"A pencil is a tool for writing."

"A pencil is a piece of wood with a yellow body and a black tip that is used for writing."

. . .

"A pencil is a writing instrument which conceals a core of lead or graphite encased within hewn wood. Its slender, circular or octagonal shape is designed to settle comfortably betwixt the webbing of the hand just behind the thumb, leaving the fore-fingers free to manipulate the delicate tip so that it scrawls legible shapes. This tip is usually pitch-black or dark grey, and in its most classical form the rest of its body is painted yellow. Additionally, some pencils bear a metallic collar on the end opposite to the tip, which affixes to the wood a piece of pink rubber. This rubber is used to erase the scrawls of lead or graphite when they are judged to be awry, and thus it is called an eraser."

A HUMAN

"A human is a person that stands upright and is thought to be more intelligent than the other great apes."

"A human is a bipedal, relatively-hairless mammal with two arms, two legs, two eyes, one nose, two ears, many white teeth, one mouth, ten fingers, ten toes and has various fleshy skin tones."

"Humans are relatively-hairless great apes with two arms, two legs, two eyes, one nose, two ears, many white teeth, one mouth, ten fingers, ten toes and has various fleshy skin tones. Human hair comes in an enormous range of styles and is often artificially died to any visible colour on the human-eyesight spectrum. Their eyes are front facing spherical orbs, predominantly coloured white, with either an amber, blue, green, grey, brown, hazel, black or in very rare cases, red. This coloration surrounds a jet-black pupil, topped with eyelashes and in some cases, bushy eyebrows. The nose has two nostrils of varying shapes and sizes, be that flat

or aquiline. Humans also have two lips, predominantly in a red colour in a half oval shape. Some of the male gender have facial hair which can range from wispy hairs on the upper lip to great beards reaching past the breastbone. Their ears are an unusual shape not found elsewhere in nature which is best described as a letter C, with an inner Y shaped structure leading to a small listening cavity..."

ADD A DROP OF METAPHOR

Unless you are educated in metaphor, you are not safe to
be let loose in the world.

ROBERT FROST

Aristotle is said to have claimed that the most adept of
communicators spoke in metaphors. He was right, because
speaking in metaphors is like the breath of a God blowing upon
a barren land, bringing whatever it touches to life.

As outlined in the previous chapter on the benefits of adding a
visual image, metaphors are especially helpful in conveying
information to yourself and others, because they allow for the
mind to visualize key concepts and ideas. Metaphors are
essentially a micro-story; a simple explanation; a novel figure of
speech; a visual replacement or a substitution which isn't meant
to be taken literally.

The images used in metaphors appeal to the primal, emotional part of the human brain which like rhetoric, can often allow their use to undermine rational thought. Given this, you should use metaphors carefully, as many a horrendous act has been obscured by their misuse, particularly those which dehumanise. The Nazi's referred to Jews as *'rats'*,[1] nationalists often refer to outsiders as *'savages'*,[2] and one particularly prominent white-supremacist would portray humans as animals by saying '...*illegal immigrants with criminal records are tonight roaming free*' to justify the use of cages in immigration detention centers.[3] When you hear these words, criticise them.

However, even the sane and peace-loving use metaphors in *spades*, we *litter* our talks with them, we *drop them here and there* into conversation. We cannot *escape* them. They are *dotted around us, everywhere*. Metaphors are used to *turn the tide* on government policy, bring a *new dawn* of charitable aid or *shower* dividends upon investors. Metaphors cross cultural boundaries; Asian cultures talk of *'saving face'* while Western cultures use the tongue in cheek term *'to cover their ass'* as protection. If metaphors were literal, the world would be a rather confusing place.

You may not even realise how frequently you use them. Each person has their own particular form of metaphoric style reflective of their personality; some prefer the kinaesthetic, mechanical style of *'taking control of the wheel'* whereas others reference nature by *'planting a seed in their mind'*. It can be advantageous to your professional advancement to identify the style you and your associates prefer to use. Identifying your own style can also help to identify communication issues, for if a colleague talks of *'hitting the target early'* whereas you reply of *'nipping it in the bud'* you are conveying a message opposite to the understanding of your companion – leading to potential conflict.

Metaphors can also be used to change beliefs and are *powerful weapons* used by political *spin* doctors. You may recall the words *'financial storm'* making headlines in 2008. To this day, no high-ranking individuals in the banking and investment industries have been punished for their crimes which left millions destitute; the use of metaphor may explain why. It is obvious there was no *storm, typhoon* or *tsunami* which *whipped through* the banking sector, merely greedy speculators who chose to ignore warnings. Yet, the storm metaphor passed on the blame and suggested it was an *act of God* or an unstoppable *force of nature*. Should the storm metaphor have been dropped and a more honest term such as 'financial crime' have taken its place, it would no-doubt have allowed for the idea of prosecution to enter into the public psyche.

On the other hand, emotionally charged metaphors are regularly used by journalists who can easily *inflame hearts* by stating how a family was *ripped apart* – when in reality nothing of the sort had occurred. We read of industries *hit* with fines, charities *pleading out* for support, or the ever-present use of the eye-rolling term of a company, group or person being *slammed* after investigation. We say violence *spreads*, as if it were an epidemic or a communicable disease. In *brighter times* we read how the economy is *flourishing*, children are *blossoming* and adults are *sitting comfortably* on *nest eggs*. Picture that image if you can without giggling.

Metaphors are therefore especially effective at suggesting viewpoints one should hold and changing the thoughts and behaviour of others. This then raises the question; what is the ideal type of metaphor? The answer is simple; if the image depicted can be understood by the primal part of the brain and across varying cultures it is an effective metaphor.

There are five distinct types of effective metaphor:

- Weather and seasonal

- Bodily acts and movement

- Food and water

- Journey and location

- Personification and Social

All metaphors are multifaceted and some stray into the realm of idiom. Some may see one statement as holding a negative connotation whereas others see it as a positive.

For weather and seasonal, Spring metaphors talk of *new beginnings* for one's life, or the beginning of a new era with the *Arab Spring*. Summer brings with it hopes for *sunny predictions* in the economy or reference to hellish *sunshine units* – a measurement of atomic fallout. Retirees enjoy their *Autumn years* whereas others dread the *last days of Autumn* of their life. Markets are advertised as a *winter wonderland* whereas a potential catastrophe is a looming *nuclear winter*. Further still we talk of *the dawn of a new day* when embarking on a new project or how *the end of the day* comes for its closing. In politics we hear of *rainbow coalitions* spreading joy, whereas job losses are *on the horizon* spreading doom and gloom. Winston Churchill toiled through *the darkest hour* where beforehand the great depression brought about *dark days* for millions of families. In the press we hear of illicit *shadowy figures* doing illegal dealings *in the shadows* or celebrities being *eclipsed* by another person's talent. All these metaphors appeal to the primal, emotional part of the human brain and allow for much imagination and interpretation.

In comparison, bodily act metaphors are often crude but effective. Conservatives attack workers by claiming they come from *the bowls of the Trade Union* as if they were faeces. Labourers in comparison claim they are being *defecated on by management* as if they were pigeons sat below each other. In psychology, Freud outlined a personality type with the metaphor of someone being *anally retentive*. Schoolchildren talk of being fed *slop* rather than the *ambrosia of the Gods*. Investments reach a *fever pitch* of buying frenzy.

Movement metaphors talk of cabinet *shuffles*, people *running amok, sitting on their laurels* or *biting the bullet*. If we wish someone good luck we say *break a leg* - a paradox if there ever was one. If we tease them we say we are *pulling their leg*, but if they *let their hair down* too much we might just *give them the cold shoulder*.

Food and sustenance metaphors are often far more pleasing to hear. We talk of business ventures being *ripe for the taking* or *dangling in front of us*. In investments we have *cash flows*, *liquidity* or if all else fails, we *freeze assets*. Reward and punishment are administered by *carrot and stick*. A loved one can be described as *the apple of my eye* despite them having the *appetite of a pig*. Politics has its *pork barrel* spending, *election sweeteners* or an undermining of the working class with claims of demands for *champagne socialism* by conservative governments which *pillage the taxman's coffers*.

Journey and location metaphors are similarly compelling as they appeal to the explore and reward part of the emotional brain, explaining why they feature such prominence in religious texts. Buddha talked of the enlightened following the *Eightfold Path*. Sikhs are taught to *seek out* a Guru. The Bible writes of *following* Christ. In the workplace, we see how a majority of people would rather *follow someone else's expedition* than *lead their own*. How often do we hear leaders describe themselves as Cookian adventurers sailing the high-seas *in search of fortune* when they *set out on a new corporate journey* only with some later caught doing *back alley deals* and giving *under the table* kickbacks.

Probably the most effective of all metaphor though is that which personifies. Disney and Pixar use personification liberally throughout its movies; *Toy Story, Beauty and the Beast* and *Wall-E* all bring to life inanimate objects to sing, dance and tell cherished tales. There's no wonder they rank among some of the most memorable movies of all time. Household items are personified in similar fashion; cookies are marketed with the *Pillsbury Doughboy*, sweetcorn is gathered by the *Jolly Green Giant* and toys are powered by the *Duracell Bunny*. Look around your home and see if you can add a personification metaphor to what you own. You may say your fireplace *calls out to you* to sit in its glow. You may feel the ice cream in your fridge *beckons* for you to eat it or perhaps you feel your car *has its own personality*. In social terms we read of the UK leaving the European Union as a *painful divorce* whilst across the world we have *sister states* engaged in sharing cultures. Who could forget the *Founding Fathers* of America?

However, having learned all these metaphors and their many appeals, consider the following sentence:

. . .

Here at ACME corporation we are branching out a strategy and laying the foundation to plant a seed in our customer's mind with the intention of hitting the ground running once our new dawn arrives in the next fiscal quarter. The new mechanisms we implement are proactive and will drive forward a revolution in growth, propelling our consumer base in record time, ultimately leading to the delivery of our unique selling point, preventing a crushing defeat by the hands of our competitors.

I forgive you if your eyes glazed over reading the above statement. That was intended.

The reason that material was so difficult to read and understand was because the metaphors were mixed. They jump from militaristic, to building, to nature, to movement, to seasonal, then on to mechanical, to mental, back to mechanical, to human, back to mechanical, to time, to movement, to militaristic and ending on a body metaphor. Yet, you have no doubt seen similar statements given by Fortune 100 companies day after day. Cynics say this mixing of metaphors is purposeful to hide the true motives of a company, others say it is caused due to death by committee where a diverse range of input is added, regardless of how confusing the end product will be.

Therefore, in your practice be wary of mixing metaphors. It is especially common to hear people talk of someone '*stepping up to the plate, running their mouth only to land in hot water*' – which really doesn't make much sense.

Knowing what you know now, you may wish to try and make your own metaphors. However, there are certain types of metaphors which should be avoided. Particularly those of a *mechanical, militaristic* or *de-humanising* nature.

For example; it is far more effective to describe a location as the *'heart'* of a city rather than the *'hub'*. It is better to describe an object with *'character'* rather than *'ease of use'*. It is more nuanced to refer to a person with *'a lighting brain and disarming smile'* rather than *'rapid communicative ability and aesthetic appeal'*. Identifying which metaphors work and which do not can be difficult at first. Try to listen to the language of the leaders around you, because they have usually developed a range of metaphors which are effective to a large group of people.

Secondly, mechanical or automatic metaphors should be avoided when discussing people, because mechanical metaphors are cold, lifeless and uncaring rather than reflective of the grand nature of human life. The use of machine metaphors is often attributed to the thinking of *Frederick Winslow Taylor* (1956 – 1915), a 20th century mechanical engineer whose seminal work *The Principles of Scientific Management* (1911) started the management consultancy industry. Despite Taylor acting as an important figure in management thinking, his work was reliant upon one singular metaphor for the description of people similar to his construction lines – *machines*. During the industrial revolution using a machine metaphor was spurred on by the thinking of the time, but in more recent times it is inappropriate, because machine metaphors are dehumanizing and serve only to diminish motivation. I have had many clients openly distain the use of mechanical metaphors from upper management. Several are frank and honest, stating they no longer feel as if they are *'cogs in the system'*, but merely *'the worn off shavings that have fallen under the machine'*. It is in my view therefore that such mechanical metaphors should be avoided at all costs and replaced with more naturalist examples. Yet, still we see workers defined as being *'part of a well-oiled machine'* in *'an inter-connected structure'* as the *'facilitators of production'*. Similar to the unthinking metaphors referring to workers as *'busy little worker bees'* or *'drones'* - none of these terms are appealing to the free-thinking individual. Workers have free will, regardless of what some management may wish to enforce upon their *'human capital'*.

Jeremy Clarkson, a world-famous motor journalist, is a master of avoiding mechanical metaphor. Whereas the usual journalist would claim the air-conditioning in a Lamborghini is underpowered, Clarkson would say *"...the air-conditioning in Lamborghinis used to be like an asthmatic sitting in the dashboard blowing at you through a straw"*.[4] Such metaphors are witty, memorable and convey the information in a way which can be understood easily across cultural barriers.

This neatly segues to car metaphors which much like their mechanical brethren should be avoided if possible, because they often work in an antiquated hierarchal manner. One is either the driver, passenger or a mechanical component under the control of another. Few people prefer to be seen as anything other than the driver of their own actions.

Other metaphors to be avoided would be those pertaining to sports. Similar to business jargon, sporting metaphors contain numerous terms which can be unknown to the non-fan. Talk of a *'sticky wicket'* may appeal to the cricket fan, but to the watcher of tennis or football it may make little sense.

War metaphors should similarly be avoided especially when discussing illness or people - unless a literal war is being fought. You may remember a time when cancer fundraising marketing material talked of *'fighting'* or *'waging war'* against cancer. No cancer patient waged war against their disease and these militaristic metaphors were found to be demoralising for the patient who was expected to militarize their body – an impossibility. Patients were told to '*keep up the fight*', '*battle on*' and '*never surrender*' - as if they had a choice. Doctors and nurses were seen as generals and conscripted allies using a range of weapons; high-powered shots, devastating laser beams and destructive lancets, rather than healthcare professionals administering medicine and compassionate treatment. Worse yet, should a patient die from cancer, loved-ones were often told the patient '*lost their battle with cancer*' almost suggesting the sufferer failed to fight hard enough and that they were weak. Thankfully through awareness campaigns, marketing material has since changed leading to a demilitarization of cancer treatment. This change has eased the suffering of patients and clearly demonstrates how even a minor change of metaphor can revolutionize an entire sector.[5]

Finally, avoid all forms of de-humanisation. Such crude and unvirtuous metaphors are the realm of the dictator, the despot and the deviant which serve only to purport one person as existing in a realm above the other. Regardless of creed, culture or circumstance we of the human race bleed the same colour when cut. There are neither '*blue-bloods*' nor '*savages*'. People cannot be '*harvested*' nor '*harnessed*' for their energies like crops or workhorses. Criminals do not '*roam free*' like animals nor are they '*monsters*' - regardless of the cruelty of their actions. No matter how much newspapers may repeat such lies, the unemployed and disenfranchised are not '*leeches*', '*bloodsuckers*' or '*parasites*' on the welfare state – taxes exist for supporting the needy via a vitally important '*security net*' and demonising such people only serves to pit one against the other, benefiting the immoral alone. Using such language will bring you neither wealth nor high-status in your community – only ridicule.

Having learned all these types of effective metaphor, try to create your own using the examples above and below using the 'stonemasonry', 'leaf' and 'manhole cover' examples as outlined earlier.

"Why I only have to look outside and I can see towering, imposing marble pillars lining our local bank akin to silent monoliths standing guard above the vaults buried deep below. These boulders, formed in the fires of our primordial days were hauled and carved by human hands into stalwart vanguards of capital. Produced by volcanoes and powers we can seldom imagine, they are reduced now to nothing but geometric patterns to keep out the vagabond, like the fingers of giants."

"I remember seeing how trees desperately resisted those violent winds, bending their trunks in unison. It was as if each one of them had accepted their fate and knew it was foolish to even attempt to resist the sheer power that a typhoon is capable of. Others, cracked and torn like strands of straw pulled from a haybale at the hands of an angry child, were scattered across the land for as far as the eye could see. Some were still airborne as they sailed like missiles through the sky. But nothing, not even that sight, compared to the fear of watching the roof above me be peeled like a tin can and hearing the scream of the storm as it hit me."

"Clouds are like a grey canvas spread across our skies, they are like a blot on the peripherals of our vision or a great cataract across our atmosphere. How I long to live in a country where the skies are clear like a forest spring or where the blue azure

found on the sandy shore of some foreign land shines from above."

Using these examples for inspiration, try to create your own metaphors or examine how objects, people, themes and concepts, etc... in the world around you are subject to their influence.

FOLLOW WITH A FACT OR AN INTERESTING POINT

Always give a speech that you would like to hear.

ANDRII SEDNIEV

The Guinness Book of World Records is an international best-seller, because people love to learn new facts and read about interesting and wonderous things. Much like hearing a visual description, learning something new aligns with the yearning for stories inherent in the human psyche. Therefore, once you have defined your object, described it visually and added a metaphor, you should then follow up with a fact or interesting point.

This often sounds more challenging on paper than it actually is, but thankfully the subconscious is a most wonderful tool and I have found students are able to drag from the depths of their memory at least one long forgotten fact, short story or glimmer of insight which can further support their talk. However, when practicing this exercise do not attempt to give a lecture on the topic, instead attempt to offer a one or two sentence statement of interest.

Consult the examples below and attempt to create your own sentence with a fact, statistic or interesting point. (*In these examples the last three parts of the practice framework have been omitted to aid with demonstration.*)

"Ancient stonemasons at the Vithalla temple in India somehow made musical stone pillars! These pillars are said to be over five-hundred years old, the same size and made from solid granite, yet each one is tuned to a specific musical note and the temple can be 'played' by hitting them with a stick!"

"The leaves of the raffia palm plant can grow up to 80 feet long, which is taller than most houses!"

"Manhole covers are especially mundane, unless you live in Japan. I remember during a holiday seeing hundreds of them decorated in vibrant colours showing landscapes, local traditions or even manga characters. Some even work as maps for travellers, pointing the way to a tourist destination and others act as meeting points for friends!"

"Perhaps you think bookbinding to be boring? Perhaps this is because we are only used to books bound in paper, card or leather. But did you know that books have been found bound in

real, human skin? It's a tad grim I know! Oh, don't worry, you're not liable to find any like that down at your local library!"

"The webcamera wasn't actually invented for video calling, it was first used to check if there was any coffee left in the Cambridge university canteen!"

"A particularly interesting fact about Abraham Lincoln is that he created an 'Air Force' forty years before the first manned flight. He created 'Balloon Force 1' which used hydrogen balloons to spy on the Confederate army."

The important thing to remember when outlining your interesting point is that it should be short, rather than a story which rambles out of control. Rambling stories are like the traveller who in deciding to take the scenic route, quickly finds himself caught in a thicket of brambles and mired down in a muddy bog; the enjoyment quickly dissipates and they long for the well-trodden path. Be sure to make your point and then move on. This can be quite difficult at first, but if you practice a little each day you will quickly improve to become a great teller of tales.

PROPOSE AND ANSWER A QUESTION

It is not the answer that enlightens, but the question.

EUGENE IONESCO

A question well stated is half solved. Yet, if you have children, the most common question you may hear is probably *'why?'*.

We are especially curious by our nature, but one thing I hear regularly from clients is that they hate being questioned. This is primarily because at work they are met with aggressive questions which demand either a yes or no answer with no room for self-expression, or they are subject to managers who would relish in the sardonic act of pointing a gestapo-esque spotlight on their victims.

Why then discuss questioning when talking to yourself? It is my view that adding a question to your thought-articulation practice can act as a miraculous way of aiding yourself in becoming more creative during moments of stress. It can also improve your recollective mental muscles. Through this effort, you will also grow your interpersonal communication skills and cultivate an ability to create a coherent response when pressed on a particularly difficult topic.

Here are eight styles of questions which you could incorporate into thought-articulation practice or your wider communication skills:

CLOSED QUESTIONS

Closed questions are the easiest to answer as these are the simplistic 'yes or no' question which almost every politician from time immemorial has been taught to avoid answering. Probably the most notorious example of avoiding answering a closed question was an interview between *Jeremy Paxman*, one of England's toughest journalists and *Michael Howard*, a member of parliament, regarding the suspension of a high-ranking prison governor. In this interview Paxman would ask Howard the same closed question: *'did you threaten to overrule him?'*, fourteen times in a row, demanding a simple yes or no answer – of which Howard would awkwardly dodge each time. Closed questions are often easy to answer. However, in your practice you should occasionally follow up your yes or no rationale with an emotional explanation, thus turning any closed questions to your own benefit.

OPEN ENDED QUESTIONS

In comparison to simple yes or no questions, open ended questions are multifaceted. They allow for the listener to give an answer which may be a mixture of a yes or no statement, supported by a series of facts or opinions. These are the *who, what, when, why* and *how* questions which if given to someone who enjoys talking or has a strong opinion, can lead down rabbit holes deep and wide. Open ended questions are excellent for examining your own opinions.

One of the finest rhetorical replies to an open-ended question was given by *Noah Sweat Jr.* (1922 – 1996), a state representative who in 1952 was asked if the State of Mississippi should continue its prohibition of alcohol:

"My friends, here is how I feel about whiskey: If when you say whiskey you mean the devil's brew, the poison scourge, the bloody monster, that defiles innocence, dethrones reason, destroys the home, creates misery and poverty, yea, literally takes the bread from the mouths of little children; if you mean the evil drink that topples the Christian man and woman from the pinnacle of righteous, gracious living into the bottomless pit of degradation, and despair, and shame and helplessness, and hopelessness, then certainly I am against it.

But, if when you say whiskey you mean the oil of conversation, the philosophic wine, the ale that is consumed when good fellows get together, that puts a song in their hearts and laughter on their lips, and the warm glow of contentment in their eyes; if you mean Christmas cheer; if you mean the stimulating drink that puts the spring in the old gentleman's step on a frosty, crispy morning; if you mean the drink which enables a man to magnify his joy, and his happiness, and to forget, if only for a little while, life's great tragedies, and heartaches, and sorrows; if you mean that drink, the sale of which pours into our treasuries untold millions of dollars, which are used to provide tender care for our little crippled children, our blind, our deaf, our dumb, our pitiful aged and infirm; to build highways and hospitals and schools, then certainly I am for it.

This is my stand. I will not retreat from it. I will not compromise."

PROBING QUESTIONS

Then there are probing questions which many enjoy asking but dislike answering. A probing question is one which attempts to outline the fundamental reasonings or rationale behind an action, opinion or reality. A probing question may be as simple as a request for more information such as *"when I finish this work, would you be happy to tell me your thoughts on it please?"* or as aggressive as those used by detectives and lawyers intent on seeking out the truth. Due to their nature in asking for the bigger picture, it is natural for people to become defensive when asked these questions, because it forces them to explain their emotions – something which I have found not many can do. Therefore, probing questions are ideally avoided when speaking to others. However, they are especially beneficial when practicing in private, because they can improve your introspective abilities.

FUNNELLING QUESTIONS

Funnelling questions are another form of investigative question. They are consecutive questions following a specific theme. Often used by journalists, lawyers and police officers who are attempting to elicit a specific answer from the questioned party they aim at undercovering hidden information. Perhaps an investigator suspects the questioned party was a criminal; the investigator would therefore ask funnelling questions which have little wriggle room for escape. A typical funnelling question scenario could be; *"...What is your occupation? Is it true you are in a large amount of debt? Are you aware of a robbery at the local jewellers? Where were you last Tuesday night? How did you get that cut on your hand?"*. Much like probing questions, funnelling questions can be especially intimidating to the one being questioned. Funnelling questions can be difficult to incorporate into extemporaneous speech unless you are attempting to answer a particularly complex problem or pursue an admission of guilt.

RECALL AND PROCESS QUESTIONS

To encourage critical thinking in yourself or an audience on a particularly demanding topic such as philosophy, religion or economics it can be advisable to ask a 'recall and process' question. These are the questions which are found during interviews or exams. The example; *'can you recall learning about the suffering of people under Communist regimes and what do you think that would be like?'* could be answered in a multitude of ways. The individual may not be able to recall learning about Communism, but they may have an opinion on the matter, which can then be questioned further to outline why they think the thoughts they do. Once again, this is an ideal example for testing your personal knowledge and identifying any substantial gaps.

LEADING QUESTIONS

Leading questions are not always negative, but they can demand obedience due to peer pressure. For example, an art critique may say *"...this is a beautiful painting, isn't it?"*, which depending on the scenario may not actually be a question; instead it would be a statement. By suggesting one abide by the opinion of the questioner, it reinforces the notion that you should answer *"yes, it is"* to either be polite or to capitulate to the opinion of someone with a realised or perceived authority on the subject. However, in most cases there is little shame in answering *"I don't think it is, because..."* and then providing an explanation as to why – assuming you provide a polite and well-articulated rationale explaining otherwise.

In general, if you are speaking extemporaneously before an audience, you can use leading questions to get them to talk about issues you have knowledge of and help them stay on track with your line of thought. Be wary however, that their overuse can make you be perceived as an aggressive boor. Leading questions are therefore not well suited for extemporaneous speech practice, but knowing how to avoid falling for their influence can protect your character.

LOADED QUESTIONS

In comparison to leading questions, loaded questions are those which have no real benefit aside discovering facts which portray the individual in a negative light. The question *"...have you stopped beating your wife, Mr. Smith?"* is a perfect example, for if Mr. Smith were to say *"no, I don't beat my wife"* he would have effectively fallen into a trap by apparently admitting he used to beat his wife. If, however he said *"I have never beaten my wife"* he would have failed to protect his image by questioning why such an allegation was made against him. When you are subject to a loaded question, never answer yes or no, instead always debunk the loaded nature of the question by calling it out as such. A better reply would be; *"...that is a loaded question intending on portraying me as a domestic abuser. I have not and never will be violent towards my partner and I am disgusted by those who commit such crimes"*. Although this answer may seem blunt, it is the best way of countering the snap emotional judgement formed by the rhetoric in this question. Again, loaded questions are not well suited for extemporaneous speech practice.

RHETORICAL QUESTIONS

Finally, you may wish to ask a rhetorical question. These are especially effective for thought-articulation or extemporaneous speech in public, as they allow for either yourself or your audience to think whilst you continue talking, as they are not expected to interrupt you with an answer. The best way to suggest a rhetorical question is to specifically state *"let me propose to you a rhetorical question..."*. If speaking in public, a rhetorical question should reinforce that both you and your audience are in agreement with the question about to be proposed.

Now that you are aware of the eight different styles of asking a question, the difficulty then is choosing which to ask and then how to answer them impromptu. Choosing how to answer a question can be quite challenging at first, because without consideration it is possible to give a technically correct answer which fails to provide the necessary information. It is like the parachutist who fell from the sky and landed in an oak tree. Having no idea which town he was in, he spotted a child in a nearby field and shouted *"where am I?!"*, only for the child to answer *"you're up a tree!"*. The answer was technically correct, but it failed to enlighten the uncomfortable parachutist.

You may also be wary of over-answering a question and letting what should be a brief comment sprawl out of control, much like the person who replies to the question *"...would you like a cup of tea?"* with the words *"Oh yes please, that reminds me of the time I was in Bavaria and wouldn't you imagine it, they had the same teacups as well and Mrs. Mavis, well she...".*

Thankfully, these examples will help you find a happy medium which both adequately answer the question and prevent your words from spiralling out of control. In your initial practice of extemporaneous speech, I would strongly suggest you initially practice leading questions and open-ended questions. You may ask something to yourself such as:

"...and can you see the burls and knots of the wood on that tree? [Silent yes]"

"How then would a world look if trees were bare and perfectly smooth, devoid of all of nature's natural ornamentation, bereft of the beauty to be found in its many twists and turns? [Open-ended answer]"

"Is not fresh water necessary for our survival? [Silent yes]"

"What then would our world be like if fresh water was as sparse as it is in the desert? [Open-ended answer]"

"Is it not obvious most students are poorly educated on the subject of money? [Silent yes]."

"Why then do we not invest more in our education in fostering knowledge of money and its many uses? Who does it benefit to keep them uneducated? [Open-ended answer]".

. . .

There is no perfect way to answer these questions. However, the cardinal sin would be to merely repeat some knowledge, an opinion or a quote heard elsewhere, which you don't truly understand. Rote repetition adds little to your knowledge or ability to express yourself. Instead, by asking a creative question, you are encouraged to formulate a creative reply. This is not to say you need give some astounding original reply.

There is nothing wrong with explaining knowledge learned from someone else, but the response you give must be said in your own words demonstrating your genuine understanding of the topic, rather than capitulating to an emotional or kneejerk response.

END WITH A GORDIAN KNOT

A talk is a voyage with purpose and it must be charted. The man who starts out going nowhere, generally gets there.

DALE CARNEGIE

The Gordian Knot was a parable associated with Alexander the Great. In the tale, a peasant Ox-cart rider was made King and in tribute to his humble origins, Midas (of later golden touch fame) was said to have bound a knot of bark around the Ox-cart frame so tightly, that it could not be unbound. This is how your thought-articulation should conclude - bringing the separate strands together into a well-tied knot.

When practicing your thought-articulation, concluding and knowing where to stop is probably the hardest thing to do, because you have no-doubt exhausted your mind especially if you regularly find your unprepared words ramble along

ed tangents. Collecting your thoughts and intertwining
many ribbons into an impenetrable Gordian knot whilst
can prove to be fiendishly trying, but it is possible.

y, it is far easier to prevent a myriad of unrelated thoughts
amassing than to entwine and funnel them into one
nt ending mid-sentence by *speaking with an end in mind*.
someone struggles to end a conversation, thought or
, it is often because they failed to abide by that chief rule.
ring from topic to theme, apology to hesitation and
ote to aphorism shows a weakness of character to the
nce which serves only to undermine the talents of the
er. If you were to be speaking in public, a speech which
emoniously burns out like a spent candle will leave the
nce waxing poetic at your expense.

e ending a thought or speech on a topic, you must have
n it with an aim in mind. Therefore, before the conclusion
ch practice session ask yourself:

'How do I wish to end?'

'What do I most wish to convey?'

'If I were asked for my opinion, what would I give?'

s can be challenging at first, especially if you are creating
v thoughts. Therefore, choose one of the following:

- Offering up your opinion for judgement and
  consideration to an imaginary audience.

- Making a 'call to action' to incentivize yourself or your

imaginary audience to follow your lead by engaging in a motivated action.

- Suggesting a question to be mulled in the subconscious of your mind for later practice.

- Recanting a recap which repeats the key points of your thought-articulation in chronological order to further bolster your memory.

- Delivering a quotation either from some expert in the field, a poetic sentence or a sage maxim which stirs your soul.

All of these ideas work well in private practice, but offering an opinion up for judgement in a public talk (which is not between friends) is ideally avoided unless you happen to be an authority on the topic. Unfortunately, this is not the way of a modern world wherein social media demands an immediate reaction at the expense of nuance, reflection and insight – often leaving the offending contemplative being ridiculed.

It is foolish to form an opinion on a topic you have little knowledge of, because this not only acts as a hindrance in changing your opinion in the future, but also outlines to any listening audience how you may quickly pass judgement on something which you lack understanding.

In comparison, it shows much courage and intellect to say '*I don't know enough to form an opinion*'. If, however, you happen to have the knowledge or qualifications necessary to impart your view then it should be offered succinctly in twenty words or less – ideally explaining why you feel as thus with a mixture of logic and emotion.

In contrast to offering an uninformed opinion, when tasked with speaking to others, it is far safer to propose a question to your audience, because it forces them to consider your points and mull them over in their own mind. Of course, if you are practicing this by yourself your audience will be your own mind, which will further aid with improving your thoughts. Oftentimes you will find the answer to the question will strike you in the middle of some random task, which you can jot down on paper to better address at a more opportune time.

If you choose to forgo the opinion and question element, a suitable ending would be a 'call to action'. This is the act of calling upon either your subconscious or your imaginary audience to change their practices, adopt new thinking or embark on new ventures. Found often in the motivational speaking and sales worlds, this is the closing statement which says to the audience that they have all the information they need to take the next step. Often when speaking to yourself, this demand will ensure you act. This can be especially beneficial if you have chosen to summarise the key learning from a book, because it instructs you to act upon its teachings.

Delivering a quotation is also an easy way to end. However, ensure you choose something relative and short which you can recite flawlessly. Choosing a poem may seem appealing when speaking to yourself, but it can be especially embarrassing if you flub your lines when speaking to others, due to the anxiety of wishing to finish talking.

Finally, the safest ending would be to summarize your practice in a few succinct words:

. . .

"In summary, stonemasonry is of great importance to the human race, because it has continued to support the upholding of our construction and the flourishing of the beauty found in design since our earliest times."

"Although you may feel as if leaves have little importance, it's clear now that we must act and ensure we follow a green energy policy to ensure their survival. The deforestation of our planet is no different from tearing out the lungs. We simply cannot survive without our green forests."

"Why do we have to decorate our streets with only greys, silvers and browns? How is our modern architecture any different from a prison toilet? If Japan in its appreciation for beauty can turn those most boring of objects, a manhole cover, into something so beautifully coloured, unique and appealing, what is stopping us aside a desire to keep our streets dull and depressing?"

LIST OF PRACTICE TOPICS

> *One important key to success is self-confidence. An important key to self-confidence is preparation.*
>
> ARTHUR ASHE

Through reading this book you have now learned:

- Why you should talk to yourself.

- How to speak like an immortal.

- How small talk results in small ideas.

- The dangers of mindless chatter, emoji overuse and swearing.

- Why you don't need to be a 'genius' to speak well.

- The importance of subvocalization and articulating your internal-dialogue.

- Why poor thought-articulation could lower your emotional intelligence.

- How your thinking impacts your speech.

- Three easy to learn rhetorical techniques.

- How to form sound opinions and recognise unsound ones.

- How you may have potentially been held back by political actors.

- How to structure your thought-articulation and extemporaneous speech practice.

As previously mentioned, in your following practice you need not cover all the structures, as there may be occasions when some (such as a visual description of an abstract concept) are unnecessary or may weaken your thought-articulation. However, it is important to practice each element whenever you can to strengthen your ability to speak unprepared, expand your mind and improve your thought-articulation.

If you are struggling for ideas of topics to discuss, consider any number of the following examples which will serve to be excellent ideas for self and group discussion:

- Acting
- Adventure

- Advertising
- Aging
- America
- Anarchism
- Animals
- Anthropology
- Archaeology
- Aristocrats
- Art
- Artificial Intelligence

- Banking
- Battles
- Bees
- Billionaires
- Biology
- Books
- Brain (the)
- Business

- Capital Punishment
- Capitalism
- Charity
- Chemistry
- Church (the)
- City Life
- College
- Colours
- Comedy
- Communism
- Computers
- Consciousness
- Conversation

- Coronavirus
- Country life
- Crime
- Culture
- Cyber attacks

- Death
- Debating
- Decisiveness
- Deep breathing
- Depression
- Devil (the)
- Dignity
- Disappointment
- Disasters
- Divorce
- DNA
- Drugs

- Economics
- Education
- Electricity
- Emergencies
- Emotions
- Endurance
- Enemies
- Envy
- Equality
- Ethics
- Etiquette
- European Union (the)
- Evolution
- Exercise

- Experiments
- Extroverts

- Faces
- Farming
- Fear
- Fiction & non-fiction
- Films
- First-aid
- Flowers
- Food
- Forgiveness
- Frankenstein's Monster
- Free speech
- Friends

- Geology
- Ghosts
- Globalisation
- God
- Gold
- Good and evil
- Gossip
- Gratitude
- Great men and women

- Habits
- Happiness
- Health
- Hearing
- History
- Homelessness
- Honesty

- Hospitals
- Humanity
- Hygiene

- Ideals
- Imagination
- Immigration
- Industrialisation
- Inspiration
- Internet (the)
- Introverts
- Inventions
- Investing

- Japan
- Jewellery
- Jingoism
- Journalism
- Joyriders
- Jury duty
- Justice

- Labour
- Landlords
- Language
- Law
- Leadership
- Leisure
- Lies
- Light
- Literature
- Lockdown (effects of)
- Logic

- Love

- Manners
- Marriage
- Mathematics
- Medicine
- Meditation
- Memory
- Mental health
- Military (the)
- Millionaires
- Mistakes
- Monetary policy
- Money
- Morality
- Music

- Nanotechnology
- Nationalism
- Nature
- Navy
- Necessities
- Newspapers
- Nonconformists
- Nuclear power

- Obesity
- Oil
- Online learning
- Opportunity
- Optimism
- Oratory
- Organ harvesting (forced)

- Organic foods
- Original thought
- Overspecialisation

- Pandemics
- Patience
- Peace
- Persistence
- Personal magnetism
- Personality
- Philosophy
- Physics
- Poetry
- Pollution
- Positive thinking
- Poverty
- Power
- Power of silence (the)
- Prejudice
- Pride
- Processed food
- Procrastination
- Pseudoscience
- Psychology
- Public speaking
- Punishment

- Quack doctors
- Quality
- Quantum computing
- Queen (the)
- Questioning
- Quiet

- Quotes

- Radio
- Railroads
- Reading
- Real estate
- Reality
- Recycling
- Relaxation
- Religion
- Remote working
- Renting
- Resourcefulness
- Rhetoric
- Risk
- Robots
- Rules

- Salesmanship
- Sanity
- Secrets
- Self defence
- Self-confidence
- Self-criticism
- Self-education
- Shakespeare
- Simplicity
- Skyscrapers
- Slang
- Slavery
- Smoking
- Social change
- Socialism

- Society
- Sociology
- Solitude
- Space
- Speaking
- Sport
- Story-telling
- Stress
- Success
- Suicide
- Sunshine
- Survival of the fittest
- Sustainability
- Sympathy

- Talking
- Taxation
- Tea
- Teaching
- Technology
- Television
- Temperance
- Terrorism
- Theatre (the)
- Theology
- Time
- Tipping
- Traitors
- Traveling
- Trees
- Trust
- Truth

- Ulterior motives
- Understanding
- Unemployed (the)
- Unionisation
- Universe (the)
- Universities
- Usefulness

- Vaccinations
- Value
- Vegetables
- Virtual reality
- Virtue
- Vision
- Vitality
- Vitamins

- Walking
- Want
- Water
- Wealth
- Westernisation
- Willpower
- Winning vs losing
- Wiretapping
- Wisdom
- Women's rights
- Worry
- Writing

- X-rays

- Yearning

- Yeast
- Yoga
- Yogis
- Yourself
- Youth

- Zeitgeist (spirit of)
- Zombies
- Zoos

The list here is clearly not exhaustive of the topics you may discuss. However, it has been carefully chosen to reflect a wide range of personal interests and global issues which will serve well to aid with developing both your understanding of the world around you and outlining any particular limitations of your knowledge.

Once you become proficient with your practice you could also attempt to challenge yourself further by using these examples:

- Speak anecdotally in a either a humorous, pathetic or tragic manner.

- Offer the pros and cons of a counter argument with either yourself, your imagination or a debating partner.

- Talk metaphorically as if you were speaking to an audience who only understood weather, food or a specific type of metaphor.

As with all your practice there will be some areas which you will not be able to speak upon. This is natural, because no person in our modern age with its untold amounts of information can be an all-knowing 'Renaissance Man'. It is a wise person who can say they hold no opinion on a matter given their lack of knowledge surrounding the issue. You should never feel ashamed to say '*I don't have an opinion on... because I don't know enough of the facts to form one*'.

CHAPTER 5

THE FORTUNE OF BEING ASKED TO GIVE A SPEECH

If you don't know what you want to achieve in your presentation your audience never will.

HARVEY DIAMOND

Being asked to give a speech demonstrates you are moving up the social strata of influence. It is proof others believe you have something worthy of note to share. It can also bring you great wealth, because often you are only one talk away from increased success. This is your moment to shine.

First and foremost, if you agree to give a speech, honour your word. Those who cancel frequently or at the last-minute cause a multitude of problems for others and are often demonised as lacking confidence, respect or care. You should also always ask what the cancelation policy is and how much notice is necessary. Be aware that in some instances you can say 'no', but due to petty office politics it will most likely not be fortuitous to your career.

Second, remember that regardless of your level of experience, giving a speech is no trivial matter. You could be a master at your trade but attempting to take the stage without any prior preparation would be foolish. If you were to purely put your faith in finding inspiration in the moment when speaking rather than relying upon previous discipline, you will find inspiration to be fleeting. Despite this, I have known of several professional speakers who have attempted to take the stage with only their memories in mind and have left audiences angry at wasting their time. This is especially rude and foolhardy if the audience is paying to see you. Proper preparation is prudent and must be practiced.

Third, be prepared for the consequences of a successful speech. You are likely to attract attention and riches if you succeed! Giving a compelling speech could change both the fortunes of yourself and the actions of your entire industry. The lady who leant her voice to that of *Siri*, the iPhone assistant, never intended her private, booth-dwelling voiceover career to lead to that of being a well-respected public speaker. The words you offer to others may take you to places you never dreamed of.

Reading this you may be reminded that we tend to underestimate our own abilities prior to learning who we really are; that is why so much of this book focuses upon the introversion of thought and extemporaneous speech through thought-articulation prior to approaching the extroversion of public speaking.

If you realize what you really want in life and have the confidence to put that desire plainly to others, you will soon find that you can get it. This is because verbal persuasion is not so much a matter of convincing your audience what they should believe, but of convincing your audience that you yourself believe what you are saying.

You must have faith, because there is something in our nature which automatically takes seriously those who take themselves seriously; we extend great generosity to those we are assured are worth listening to and this is only achieved through clear thought-articulation.

WRITING A SPEECH

Designing a presentation without an audience in mind is like writing a love letter and addressing it: To Whom It May Concern.

KEN HAEMER

A great speaker doesn't just give their audience what they want to hear. A great speaker gives them what they need to hear in a palatable manner. Anyone can speak, but only those who have quietly listened, studied and observed the needs of their audience can say the right things in the right way.

Assuming you accept responsibility for giving a talk you will have to embark upon writing a speech or planning a presentation (unless you choose to have it written for you which will be commented on later in the chapter). There are many excellent books written on speechwriting and presentation techniques, therefore this section shall only be a brief overview of what I have found to be the most accessible framework and is in no-way a comprehensive guideline.

When planning a speech or talk, you should follow the thought-articulation and extempore style which you will now be well versed with, along with the additional support of what is known as the *Ethos, Logos, Pathos* structure. These Latin names could be simply translated as *Ethics, Emotion* and *Logic*:

- *Ethos*: This is your credibility, experience and the reason why people should listen to you. It should explain why you have been chosen, but should be articulated in such a way that it isn't a brag, more-so it's a recommendation of how your knowledge can help your audience.

- *Pathos*: This is an appeal to emotion through visuals, metaphors and rhetorical devices. Your improved thought-articulation skill will be especially beneficial here.

- *Logos*: The logic of your talk. These are your findings, your evidence and your suggested contributions.

Charitable appeals are the masters of abiding by the *Ethos, Pathos* and *Logos* structure:

- *Ethos*: They begin with an opening statement such as: '...*this is an appeal on behalf of the Red Cross*' establishing their credibility, experience and rationale for attention.

- *Pathos*: They follow the opening with emotive

imagery, stories and metaphors emphasising the
struggle the needy have to overcome.

- *Logos*: They end on an appeal for your support,
  outlining how past financing has been beneficial and
  how your donation will be used.

Using the *Ethos, Logos* and *Pathos* structure is similar to how
you will have been taught at school. For chemistry, you were
taught by your chemistry teacher who was the local expert on
the topic (ethos), they would inspire you by showing visual
descriptions of chemical substances (pathos), only to then end
with the facts (logos). However, if your chemistry tutor had
merely burned some litmus paper during the lesson, rather than
dipping it in acid and explaining what the change in colour
meant, there would have been little to learn. Therefore, you
cannot write an impactful speech if your message lacks a goal to
achieve and you must always ask yourself how each sentence
links back the chief aim.

Before planning what you intend to say, you must first examine
exactly what your speech intends to achieve. Ask yourself:

- Is it to motivate?

- Is it to inspire?

- Is it to warn or inform?

- Is it to entertain, promote or persuade?

- Perhaps you have a eulogy to deliver for a funeral.

- Or maybe it's a celebration award speech beguiling someone's success.

Without knowing exactly what you intend to convey, you cannot speak with an aim in mind. Knowing this aim is the most important part of your speech.

STRUCTURING A SPEECH

Once you have identified the aim of your speech, commit all of the information you can recollect onto paper. This works especially well with your goal written in the centre of the page with a spider diagram denoting how the knowledge identifies back to the objective. The sprawling information can eventually be arranged into a skeleton outline consisting of the main objective at the top with descending logically connected points. Some find imagining the script being akin to a nervous system feeding back to the brain being the main point as useful.

After having written all the information you can muster and researching more if necessary, you can then begin questioning the information to include and omit. This is achieved by identifying the *knowledge gap* between you and your audience. If your audience is as learned as you in your particular niche this may not be a problem. However, if you are speaking more widely, consider your knowledge as *Graham Davies'* explained in *The Presentation Coach* (2010) - akin to observing a pyramid from different viewpoints. Up close the golden tip may be obscured, whereas from far away the intricate details are easily missed. Similarly, the structural supporting knowledge of your talk may be obvious to you but unknown to others. It may not be necessary to outline every step to the top and each hidden tunnel, but it is necessary to show them the gleaming point which is usually the very reason why you were invited to speak.

This trimming of unnecessary information can be particularly difficult, but submitting your knowledge to scrutiny and asking which themes can be the most easily explained is usually the ideal choice. If you cannot explain a point succinctly, your audience is similarly liable to misunderstand what you say.

An excellent exercise is to submit your points to a mock question and answering session:

- What is your audience liable to ask for more information on?

- Which concepts are regularly misunderstood?

- What would your competition say of your statements and how would you rebuke them?

- Are there points in your talk which you cannot explain further?

- Are there themes you can explain with a singular image, a poem, a story, metaphor or in less words?

- How can you summarise this knowledge, what metaphors or visual imagery can you use?

- Do you need props, diagrams or pictures or are you confident enough in your speaking abilities?

- Pyramids also have internal tunnels which can bypass

hidden chambers; is there some knowledge you are
privy to which although interesting, can be bypassed?

Taking the effort to ask all these questions will ensure you talk
in a *top-down manner* by outlining the information you feel is
most relevant. Furthermore, having this mental rehearsal will
more-often-than-not save you from the stress of thinking on your
feet during a real Q&A.

DRAFTING YOUR SPEECH

Ideally your draft speech should first be written out in full and
then summarised into bullet points allowing you to speak
extemporaneously. Reading verbatim from a complete
manuscript is best left to those making political statements,
claims of innocence or delivering some vitally important
information.

Having decided upon the necessary information to include,
write the final message or closing line of your speech first. This
may seem counterproductive, but by following this rule it
ensures your speech does not meander and you instead speak
with an end in mind. Much as an arrow is drawn back from the
string of a bow, when let loose it has three possible outcomes; it
will either fall short, overshoot or hit its mark. To hit the mark
with your speech, you must act like the arrow and progress in a
strong, linear line which does not deviate away from your main
point. Much like our aforementioned pyramid or skeletal
structure and nervous system, each statement you make should
logically progress from the other in a sequential order.

Upon writing the final line of your speech, a compelling
opening line should be your next priority. One of the most
impactful opening lines I heard was given by an NHS nurse at a

medical forum which began with; *'By the time this talk is over, three in ten of you will have developed cancer cells in your body - that's why we need more funding.'* The temperature in the room plummeted, all conversation stopped and she immediately had the attention of everyone in the room such was the morbidity of the claim. Her opening statement outlined exactly what the topic was concerning, why the talk was being given and why people should listen, because it spoke to the emotions of her audience.

Creating a compelling opening statement is a difficult exercise to outline, because only you know the topic of what you wish to talk about. Therefore, consider these examples to create an attention-grabbing introduction:

- An impressive statement.

- An emotional story.

- A rhetorical question.

- A commentary on relevant local news.

- A promise to add value.

- A do or die situation.

- A statement of the facts.

- A push for change.

- A request for support.

When writing the remainder of your speech it is best to deliver your information in three parts; the introduction, the main body and the conclusion.

In the introduction it may be necessary to support your status if you have not been introduced by a master of ceremonies. Explaining briefly to your audience why you have been invited, the position you hold and the passion you have for your message is an excellent way to establish both a personal brand and credibility in the eyes of your audience. This once again is the *Ethos* and has been used by great speakers for time immemorial.

When planning your introduction, I do not recommend you outline the points you intend to cover, because your audience will most likely become disenchanted until you talk about the topic they are looking forward to hearing. Instead moving swiftly on is ideal.

When you have chosen the information to include in your introduction it should again be submitted to the harshest critics of your internalised Q&A.

THE MIDDLE OF YOUR SPEECH

The *Pathos*, or the middle of your talk should contain the thought-articulation elements you have learned thus far. To build upon your persuasive abilities you must again write for your audience. Giving a talk on joys to be found cooking a prime rib steak wouldn't be digestible to an audience of vegans.

Assuming you know your audience, you should attempt to pull their heartstrings by talking in phrases which matter to them. If there is a fear of redundancy, it would be foolish to talk about the future of working with the company. Instead it would better serve you to inspire your audience to invest in improving their skills. Similarly, if the company is growing exponentially, the bearish in your audience may want to hear a word of caution against complacency. It's always best to check with the organiser and ask what they would like to hear.

Remember also to use the metaphors your audience is liable to resonate with. Technology types may talk of '*connecting*' with each other, a charity may say they want a '*heart to heart*' meeting whilst those in finance will probably talk of '*capitalising*' on their assets. I once worked with a managing director of a bank who used the metaphors:

"*...Words are like your capital. If you don't have enough available you can't invest in yourself. We all have a phrase bank which is locked up, but it's getting access to those phrases which add value to yourself. To grow in this industry, you need to invest in your assets and compound your abilities, because if you don't, you'll stay at the bottom of the charts just like everyone else.*"

To further persuade your audience, don't be ashamed of admitting a mistake, because it can disarm those who hold a preconceived judgement. I once worked with an executive of a food production company who late in his career foolishly prioritised suggestions from his family on new goods to put into production, rather than listening to the results of customer surveys. Sales of the unpopular product were abysmal, but accepting responsibility and explaining the mistake to his team demonstrated humility and leadership.

Finally, you could consider a work-safe joke. Be wary though as these are especially treacherous waters to tread. If done well you could lighten the hearts of your audience and bring them out of a slumber during particularly stressful periods, if done poorly it could cost you your position. Also, be extremely cautious when referencing the 'running gag' in your industry. It may be unwelcome news to the current boardroom. It is painful to hear a joke fall flat, but even worse to have to explain it to a concerned senior figure.

ENDING YOUR SPEECH

Lord Mancroft once quipped '...*a speech is like a love affair. Any fool can start it, but to end it requires considerable skill*'.

Having initially written your closing message, created a compelling opening micro-statement and given your audience middle, your conclusion should come naturally to you.

In my experience, a first impression is not as important as the final emotional impact, because although a first impression can be repaired, improved or even restated through impassioned speech a weak ending devoid of emotional impact which doesn't rest on the mind will leave the speaker's topic soon forgotten and their work unfinished. This is the promising speech which fizzles out, the compelling book with the hollow characters or the show which ends with people taking to the internet to complain. All failed to create a satisfactory emotion which fed the audience's needs for a satisfying conclusion.

Much like any fine book or essay, the conclusion should not offer any new information unless it is a sales pitch and unlike movies which have the permission to end on a cliff-hanger, a formal talk should leave the audience with the necessary information to act.

As a note on making more droll information come alive; if you wish to inform the audience of a fact give it to them in the form of a story. If you have a statistic, turn it into a joke. If you want to make a point, turn it into an example. Very few audiences enjoy slide after slide of PowerPoint.

Once your manuscript has been written and summarised, your bullet points should be written on index cards in a clear, large font with adequate space between the lines for last-minute changes. Ensure to number the index cards in sequential order. There is nothing more terrifying for even a regular speaker than to flip a speech-card only to see the end card ten minutes early. Also, if you are due to present on a stage do not allow your speech cards to be shown as you walk to the podium, because this will draw the attention of your audience away from your smile. Instead, keep them in your breast pocket. There is no shame in practicing at home how to gracefully remove them from your clothing – I have seen at least one speaker struggle with cards stuffed into a pocket with an opening several inches smaller than the cards inside them, leaving him wrestling with his own suit jacket.

Once your speech is over you may be liable to have to answer unexpected questions. I believe a Q&A is one of the most valuable parts for reflecting upon your speech, because if the audience asks clarification for points which you feel were adequately explained, it may be that your clarification wasn't so adequate after all. If possible, take notes during this opportunity. If you do not happen to know the answer to a question be honest and state *'I don't know the answer to that, but if you would like to give me your contact details after the talk I'd be more than happy to find out for you'*. Try to avoid saying *'that's a good question'* as this is an answer often used by those who are in reality merely stalling for time – people have grown wary of hearing it. Offering silent contemplation can show far more respect than jumping straight into speech.

Finally, in 1888 circus master *P.T Barnum* of *The Greatest Show on Earth,* found that no vaudeville act with all its bells, whistles and prancing ponies could hold audience attention for longer than 12 minutes. Yet, even now modern management are confused that staff struggle to persevere through their third hour-long meeting of the day. If you intend to talk, make it short. Give your audience what they would like to hear, even if it's information they don't want to know.

SHOULD I HIRE A SPEECH WRITER?

If you wing it when speaking, you'll get wing it results.

ARVEE ROBINSON

There is a contentious topic amongst communication coaches; whether one should hire a speech writer or slave over creating their own material.

Purists argue it is immoral to read someone else's words as if they were your own. They see such sacrilege as fooling the audience. Some coaches may worry about clients reading verbatim and sounding like automatons – which I can partially agree with. Others see the advantage of hiring professionals, because not everyone has a masterful flourish with the pen. I however sit somewhere in-between, because a majority of my clients are CEO's, visionaries and similar high-net worth individuals who understand the importance of delegating responsibility to others in effort to better invest their time and skills elsewhere. In my view, it can be worthwhile to hire a professional speech writer who will work directly with you to leave the greatest impact upon your audience, especially if you are to speak with a teleprompter in sight.

This then raises the question; what should you look for and avoid when hiring a speech writer?

Chiefly, avoid hiring a speech writer who writes outside of your industry or ability. One of the most common mistakes I see business leaders make is hiring big-name political speech writers who write for Kings, Queens and heads of state to provide them with a script for a comparatively small forum. The speech is masterfully written, weaving poetic metaphor and convincing rhetoric into beautiful prose. All seems a success, until a mistake is made or question and answering begins, whereupon it becomes clear to the audience that the language used in the script was far beyond the capabilities of the speaker. Feeling tricked, the audience begins to doubt the speaker's true credibility. They question, if the speaker were such a master of the English language, why are their thoughts so disjointed once speaking impromptu? Can they be trusted? Did they mean what they said? What's going on behind the scenes?

Given this, when looking for a speech writer, ascertain if they have worked with people from your particular industry or niche. Further still, ask for recommendations and references which are easily found nowadays on LinkedIn. If the writer is a new talent, ask to see their portfolio; there are many talented writers waiting to be discovered by a first client.

As a general rule, a competent speech writer will ask for examples of previous talks you have given or examples of how you write, think and speak. Using this knowledge, they will provide you with a speech which resembles your particular style and uses words and phrases which are part of your daily lexicon. What they provide to you should read naturally to you, allowing for you to easily correct yourself should you lose your place during your talk, because sometimes less is more.

SHOULD I MEMORISE MY SPEECH?

Let us not burthen our remembrance with a heaviness that's gone.

WILLIAM SHAKESPEARE

Several years ago, I was hired by a pharmaceutical company to produce a video narration for a medical procedure concerning *'idiopathic hypereosinophilic syndrome'*. To this day, I can remember the entire script and its complicated medical terminology by heart. I can recall the treatment, the medication suggestions and the patient aftercare pointers and for some unknown reason, I can recite it at will. However, despite being able to deliver the script as confidently as any doctor, I have no understanding of any of it. The words were memorised by rote, it was not *understood*. If I were to be questioned on the matter, I could not answer anything concerning it. Therein lies the problem of memorisation by rote – it doesn't equate to true understanding.

Throughout my life and professional career, I have met a small number of savant-like individuals with uncanny memories who can seemingly recite entire books at whim. To some, they can often appear as if they are titans of intellect able to discuss a great deal of topics and theories. Yet, it is quite obvious how once they are put under questioning to explain the nuances of their repetitions all coherency of thought eventually breaks down unless it has been studied fastidiously. Much like in *The Wizard of Oz*; the curtain is pulled back exposing but a mere man pulling levers and whistling bells which can only do so much.

Committing your speech to the banks of your memory is a beneficial exercise, but it should not be done for the aim of producing rote repetition. The ideal way to memorise a speech is to internalise the key points to be expanded upon and then submitting them to a private Q&A. This is best achieved by recording a recital of the key points and then listening to those ideas on repeat. After several listening sessions, attempting to speak along with the recording should follow. Listening, reciting and then pausing the recording to expand with further thought-articulation is the ideal complete form of practice.

If you still struggle with coining fresh speech after your key points, I would not yet advise on contemplating how best to apologise to your host. Much as viewing fine art enriches the mind so too can the reading of masterpieces of poetry or literature. I often find my mind to be inordinately more expressive after reading some classical masterpiece before speaking or writing. Consultation with books on poetry, fiction and stories concerning the realm of your talk are especially beneficial in inspiring expressiveness even under pressure. One exercise I have found to be beneficial is the reading of some masterful piece of literature the night before a talk. Allowing

SPEAK YOUR WAY TO WEALTH

the prose to seep into my subconscious as I sleep often causes its influence to spring forth in my hour of need.

Finally, you will find that should all other exercises fail you, the adrenaline from the spotlight will force you to speak if you have persevered with your speech practice gifting you the right words at the right moment.

LEARN FROM THE NOBEL LAURATES

Words were not given to man in order to conceal his thoughts.

JOSÉ SARAMAGO

The Nobel prize is almost always awarded to the finest minds of our generation. There are numerous categories available for accolade; from science, literature, the arts and others which we need not cover in detail. Yet across the spectrum of topics there is one common theme; the winner of these accolades has mastered the art of creative thought in their particular field. It was consistent experimentation, perpetual persistence and the effort of outside the box thinking, even at the expense of 'discovery by accident', which has awarded them fame and fortune.

However, despite the prestige awarded which has the potential to change the world, Nobel prize laurates can often be shy and retiring people who avoid the limelight and for good reason. It is not uncommon for a laurate to be a poor public speaker. They may have invested decades in the same environment, surrounded by the same peers having conversations comprised of thoughts so advanced that their translation into the common tongue is seldom possible. Others abstain from communication, because their work takes priority. In rare cases, so are so insular that their verbal communication skills are their weakest abilities. Many a mathematical genius has refused awards, interviews and media appearances merely because they lacked the ability speak outside of their cherished numbers.

Yet, despite the differences in vocation, one thing that all Nobel Prize winners agree with is the importance of always carrying a notebook and pen with them at all times; for inspiration may strike at any moment and if not recorded it will soon vanish like the afterimage of a lightning bolt; it may be that the line you quickly scribbled, unaware of its full significance at the time, is the one you are remembered for.

You may not be lucky enough to attend a 'Nobel Minds' round table event held in the esteemed Grunewald Hall, but you can view them online. If you do, you will note how each Laurate has before them a notebook and pen, which will be used relentlessly throughout the discussions, as the mutual exchanging of minds from varying disciplines has the potential to stimulate both the subconscious and conscious mind into creating new and vibrant ideas.

As with every principle herein, I practice what I preach. This very book was primarily written on park benches, upon street corners, and even in the middle of shops. The mind's meteorologists are unreliable; one never knows when inspiration will rain down. And if left unwritten or uncaptured, those torrents of inspiration will evaporate back from whence they came.

HOW AND WHERE TO PAUSE

Well-timed silence hath more eloquence than speech.

MARTIN FRAQUHAR TUPPER

Comedians often get bigger laughs from a pause than a punchline. Paradoxically then, one of the finest ways to improve how you speak is to *speak less*. By that I do not mean merely to be curt or succinct in your words (yet it can be advisable in some situations). I refer to one of the more difficult elements of speaking; knowing when and how to pause.

In writing we pause with comma's, full stops and semicolons, and although it's also possible to write in italics to strongly emphasise something for consideration, if you try to italicise your body and lean sideways for emphasis when speaking you'll look rather silly. The emphasis of your words will therefore either come from the tone of your voice or the way you pause.

Despite this, silence can be agonizing even for the most experienced speaker. Yet, nowhere is eloquence and gravitas more manifest than those two to three seconds of nothingness, because your silence can't be misquoted.

A pause is not something we pay attention to during everyday speech. Often, we pause to take a breath, to catch our thoughts or to allow our words to permeate the minds of our listeners. It is to say to them 'do you understand me?'.

A speech without pause is nothing more than noise; a Morse-code delivered by voice which is robotic and wearisome to listen to. Yet, giving yourself or your audience even half a second extra to think can be incredibly beneficial to your mental clarity and their mutual understanding.

Knowing that pausing is important may also explain a common complaint I receive from my clients – they find it fiendishly difficult to read their written scripts aloud and still sound natural. Why? Surely their own words should come effortlessly to them. Unfortunately, to read aloud and sound as if one were speaking naturally is the backbone of acting. It is difficult, because we do not know where to pause. If you try to pause at every comma or at the end of every sentence, the speech is liable to sound unnatural. Comparatively, if tasked with explaining the topic in their own words, the speaker will usually pause in the right place.

Until someone is able to internalise the words as their own, a rote narrated presentation will often sound stilted and halting due to a predictable cadence and irregularity of pauses. The reality is that television announcers, actors and audiobook narrators like myself spend years attempting to avoid sounding fake and predictable when speaking words which someone else has written for us.

There are therefore two forms of pauses used when speaking; *grammatical* and *rhetorical*. Grammatical pauses are the commas, the full stops and the gaps between lists which are ignored by actors or speakers trying to memorise a script and to repeat it in a naturalistic way.

On the other hand, rhetorical pauses are points where we pause naturally for emphasis during conversation. When practicing these, a pause between 0.5 to 3 seconds will seem natural to your audience. Anything longer than 7 seconds however should be avoided, unless you are milking a crowd for laughs or want to appear like a dictator.

For grammatical pauses, pause *after*:

1. The nominative phrase.
2. The objective phrase in an inverted sentence.
3. The emphatic word or clause of force.
4. Each member of a sentence.
5. The noun when followed by an adjective.
6. Words in apposition.

For grammatical pauses, pause *before*:

1. The infinitive mood.
2. Prepositions (generally).
3. Relative pronouns.
4. Conjunctions.
5. Adverbs (generally).
6. An ellipsis.

Here are some examples taken from classical literature. Take note of the numbers used during each pause and reference them with the grammatical pause list above.

1. The passions[8] of mankind[1] frequently[3] blind them.
2. With famine[10] and death[2] the destroying angel came.
3. He exhibits[4] now and then[4] remarkable genius.
4. He was a man[5] contented.
5. The morn[6] was clear[12], the eve[6] was clouded.
6. It is prudent[8] in every man[7] to make early provision[8] against the wants of age[10] and the chances[8] of accident.
7. Nations[11] like men[6] fail[8] in nothing[9] which they boldly attempt[11] when sustained[8] by virtuous purpose[10] and firm resolution.
8. A people[12] once enslaved[1] may groan[12] ages[8] in bondage.
9. Their diadems[12] crowns[8] of glory.
10. They cried[3] "Death[8] to the traitors!"

Of course, following this guideline can be quite difficult for the majority of speakers and you are certainly not expected to memorize the rules above! If you try to pause after each of these rules, your words will still sound stilted and unnatural, because everyone speaks differently.

To demonstrate the importance of abiding by rhetorical pauses, remember that a natural pause is used after a key word or phrase when one wishes to emphasize an emotion or point necessary to build suspense or understanding. Whereas a grammatical pause is purely to abide by written linguistic structures.

Read the following text (*William Faulkner's speech at the Nobel Banquet at the City Hall in Stockholm, December 10, 1950*) aloud, abiding by the grammatical pauses (commas), then read the second example with the rhetorical pauses (dashes) and see which works best for you. You can then combine the two and make your own variant.

"I feel that this award, was not made to me as a man, but to my work, a life's work in the agony of the sweat and the human spirit. Not for glory and least of all, not for profit. But to create out of the materials of the human spirit, something which did not exist before."

"I feel / that this award / was not / made to me as a man / but to my work / a life's work / in the agony / of the sweat / and the human spirit / Not for glory / and least of all / not for profit / But to create / out of the materials of the human spirit / something / which did not / exist / before."

WORDS TO EMPHASISE

To sway an audience, you must watch them as you speak.

C. KENT WRIGHT

Knowing which words to emphasise will serve you well in adding a melody and a level of gravitas to your speech. By emphasising the correct words, you not only allow for your words to be understood, but they also carry clear instructions for what the audience is to expect or do.

Some people tend to simply increase the volume of an emphasised word; this can backfire by sounding aggressive. Instead, *lean into the word* by slowing down, stretching the word as if it were made of rubber and then adding a micro-pause after the emphasised word. Try this with the examples below:

- *I* will give this talk – Means *you* will give the talk.

- I *will* give this talk – Means you *will* give the talk (*rather than not give it*).

- I will *give* this talk – Means you will give it (*for free*).

- I will give *this* talk – Means you will give *this particular* talk.

Of further importance is the subtle nuance of *prosody,* or the inflection given to a word to emphasise a particular meaning.

Some Asian, Australian, New Zealand and American accents have a natural rising inflection which to many listeners sounds as if each sentence ends in a question, unfortunately undermining confidence to non-native ears. If you are speaking outside of those particular countries, I would strongly suggest ending each statement on a downwards inflection. This is easily practiced by copying the inflection as outlined below and substituting your own words or phrases:

- Yes ~- Questioning (*Yes?*)

- Yes →- Accepting (*Yes, please.*)

- Yes ⌐- Confidence (*Yes, I'm certain.*)

Did you notice how on the final '*Yes*' the downwards inflection gave your voice more gravitas? This is a commonly used technique by all professional speakers to sound confident in their statements.

However, be wary of ending each sentence with the same inflection, because this sounds unnatural and will often leave you sounding like a newscaster, rather than a natural speaker.

HOW TO EXPRESS EMOTION

People will forget what you said, people will forget what you did, but people will never forget how you made them feel.

There is a language of emotions alongside the language of ideas. Don't believe me? Stand before a mirror like a mime and talk on a topic you hold dear to yourself in silent body language alone and you will soon find your passions will swell as you attempt to express emotion through your gestures. Your arms will spring into action, your eyebrows will contort themselves and you will bite down on your teeth as you silently lock eyes with your own in effort to portray the emotion in your speech. Yet, despite this, many inflict upon their audiences a sense of disparity between their carefully chosen words and poor emotional delivery, leaving them judged not by what they said, but how it was said.

How often have you sat through a speech devoid of emotion, which was dry, monotone and lacking life? Knowing how to impart a genuine emotion towards your chosen topic is a crucial part of your practice towards mastery of speech.

The first change to make, as mentioned before, should be a general avoidance of reading aloud from a written speech, because the heart and mind quickly become misaligned and almost machine-like.

Secondly, orating another's words with emphasis is fiendishly difficult. Yet, even the most monotonous public reader, when placed with friends, has a voice filled with tone, volume, pitch and energy. When talking amongst friends it is the thoughts which come before the words, leading to a rich and vibrant use of enthused emotion. In comparison, reading aloud causes an overreliance on emotionless written structure, grammatical pauses and awkward pacing.

An issue which faces some speakers, especially those involved in corporate negotiation and venture capitalism, is a stone-faced stoicism akin to professional poker players. They dare not flinch lest they show their hand. Thus, when called upon to express passion they struggle to express their zeal, leaving their audience unimpressed by an apparent lack of conviction.

If you relate to this problem, you have most likely subdued your emotions to the extreme and must therefore practice the reverse. Here are several exercises which may help:

CASTING BACK THE MIND

One exercise involves casting the mind back to a particular moment which was filled with the ideal emotion and applying the once-felt emotion to the present. For example, *Cicero* (106 -

43 B.C.) wrote that one should attempt to remember a sorrowful event such as the passing of a family pet, to bring about sadness when talking on a mournful topic. You could also recollect a successful business deal or time with friends to bring about joy. Despite being first described by *Cicero*, this method is now primarily known the *Stanislavski Technique*.

A, E, I, O, U

If the recollection of emotional memories does not suffice, another even simpler exercise is to speak the vowels (A, E, I, O, U) with varying emotions. Uttering the vowels with fervour, be it ferocious or joyful, is beneficial because it allows you to vocalize emotion even in the absence of a coherent meaning.

THE TWO-MINUTE RANT

An exercise often employed in the acting spheres is the 'two-minute rant / thank / celebration'. In this, the actor spends two minutes whipping themselves into an emotional frenzy to the extreme to stimulate physiological changes such as a rapidity of heartrate or the production of hormones. I know of one public speaker who will give himself an ardent award acceptance speech before going on stage to energise his performances.

LISTEN TO MUSIC

Another beneficial practice is simply listening to music. In Japan, train stations and shopping centres often have soothing music and birdsong playing lightly in the background to calm stressed office workers. Compare this to the intrusive music played in Western malls - all intended on preventing the mind from focusing on rational thought and the expense one is paying. If you find you are struggling to muster a particular emotion, listening to music you enjoyed during your teenage years will often stimulate the brain to recollect long dormant thoughts, hormones and emotions. It is surprisingly effective.

SPEAK TO SOMEONE NEW

Another excellent exercise is attempting to describe the topic at hand to various imaginary audiences. Ask yourself, how would you deliver the topic to a group of children, a new recruit, a friend, a boss or a government panel? How would you speak as if you were wounded, or had been given the green light on a feature film with a limitless budget?

USE AN ADJECTIVE OR TWO

Finally, there are numerous emotional adjectives which work well in communicating the emotion you wish to express. Try using some of the examples below to see how they can influence the way you impart emotion into your speech.

POSITIVE EMOTION ADJECTIVES

Agreeable, amazed, animated, attractive, beautiful, bold, brave, bright, cheerful, clever, comfortable, delightful, encouraging, excited, festive, free, fresh, gentle, hopeful, jolly, kind, loving, open, optimistic, pleased, proud, supportive, sympathetic, warm, wonderful.

NEGATIVE EMOTION ADJECTIVES

Aggravated, annoyed, awful, bitter, chilly, depressed, dirty, disgruntled, disgusted, dreadful, evil, guilty, heavy, hostile, hurtful, irritated, nasty, obnoxious, oppressive, overbearing, pessimistic, resentful, sarcastic, sardonic, tearful, tense, terrible, tired, ugly, weak.

DESCRIBING OTHERS' EMOTIONS

Accepting, ambivalent, anxious, awestruck bashful, calm, candid, cautious, composed confident, cool, earnest, easy, easy-going even-handed, horrified, indifferent, intelligent, mysterious, neutral, non-partisan, passive, political, pragmatic, quizzical, religious, reserved, satisfied, secretive, secular, shy, strong, surprised, tranquil.

Do not be dismayed if you cannot turn the zeal in your mind into reality during your impromptu practice. Even the finest actors are rarely able to produce a compelling improvised scene upon a first, second or third attempt. With practice comes performance.

BREAK THE ANCIENT ROMAN RULES

The human body is the best picture of the human soul.

LUDWIG WITTGENSTEIN

Have you ever wondered why ancient Roman Senators often struck those particular statuesque poses when speaking in the senate? It wasn't just to impart a vision of grandeur; these grand stances were a necessity to fix their movement due to a decree which banned senators from learning pantomime due to the effectiveness body language had in convincing a jury. This is a rule you must break when you talk - you must use your body language to great effect.

Modern science shows us that the eyes have twenty-two times the amount of nerves as the ears, thus a speech devoid of body language could be twenty-two times less effective than one with. It would be sabotage to speak without gestures.

I am of the belief it is best to take things to the extremes in your practice, then dial them back to normality in your performances. You should therefore emulate a Shatner-like thespian by gesticulating wildly in your practice using the exercises below:

- *The Puppet* – Imagine your arms are hanging on strings like a marionette. The puppet master pulling the strings flails your arms around in a highly theatrical fashion as you speak. Make this as wide and comical as you wish. Bring down your hand in a forceful sweeping gesture to emphasise a point, or throw your arms open to call attention to your audience.

- *The Distant Orator* – Imagine you were speaking to an audience who were seated far, far away who had to judge your emotion by your body language. Start your gestures off at a normal speed, then slow them down to an eventual pause. Your grandiose movement and final stance should reflect the emotion you wish to convey.

- *The Mime* – Practice communicating in total silence with only your natural gestures available to emphasise an important point.

There are also five styles of gestures you can use which will further emphasise key points. Try practicing each style and see how they complement what you wish to convey.

- *Metaphorical gestures* – One hand marching in front of the other to show progress / spatial use to demonstrate 'before and after' / the linking of the fingers to suggest working together.

- *Illustrative gestures* – Playing the clarinet / drinking coffee / rubbing temples.

- *Signalling gestures* – Thumbs up / crossed hands / specific culturally important gestures.

- *Symbolic gestures* – Universally understood gestures / hand on heart / praying.

- *Beat gestures* – The movement of the hands to emphasise the natural rhythm of speech.

These exercises are a little over the top, but not only do they serve to force your body language outside of your usual comfort zone, but larger gestures will also act well in hiding your shaking hands, preventing you tugging at your clothes or simply wringing your palms due to nerves. I fully appreciate that you may be uncomfortable at first, but you will eventually notice a dramatic change in your natural speaking rate, cadence and an ability to inflect emotion onto your key words with their use. *However, once again: you are not expected to gesticulate like this when speaking normally!*

As this book is primarily concerned with improving thought-articulation it shall not go into any further detail regarding the ideal practices of body language. However, there are three simple rules which if abided by will enormously improve your skills.

Firstly, when speaking ensure not to spade or splay your fingers, instead your palms and fingers should be held in a graceful curve much as found on the hand of Michelangelo's 'David'.

Second, try not to allow both hands to mirror their gestures too frequently as this can often prove distracting to an audience.

Finally, when gesturing it is best practice to ensure your palms are slightly upturned as this demonstrates openness and honesty. Studying the figure-of-eight movement will aid with creating an elegant, flowing and natural gesture with upturned palms. Start by initially moving from the wrist, then the elbow and finally the shoulder as if mimicking a sideways figure of eight pattern.

It is also worthwhile to study the body language of actors, politicians and professional public speakers for a more detailed visual guide to further instruction.

However, excluding during your practice sessions, avoid over-exaggeration. Those with *helicopter-hands* which whirl and spin around erratically can often be distracting, invade the personal space of others or vanish off-camera when presenting online. If this is an issue, tie an elastic band around your middle and little finger which will act as a reminder to subdue your gestures.

Finally, in all instances gesture from the hips upwards. Ensure that your feet remain flat on the ground and that you don't lean to either side with your hips. It can be rather disconcerting to see someone wiggle and jive their body from the hips down when delivering a talk – unless they are a Yogi demonstrating how to practice standing yoga.

CHAPTER 6

PROFESSIONAL PUBLIC SPEAKING

Words have incredible power. They can make people's hearts soar, or they can make people's hearts sore.

DR. MARDY GROTHE

Having reached this far in the book, you have probably thought about speaking professionally. If you pursue this lucrative career, you may make a rousing speech heard by millions across the world and your figure stood centre stage stood in the spotlight could be the culmination of years of practice. It can be one of those career defining moments where your well-chosen words delivered in earnest may stand the test of time to be quoted and remembered by hundreds, if not thousands for years to come.

Therefore, before beginning to plan your career as a public speaker, one of the simplest rules to remember is that in the modern age audiences no longer expect the grandiloquence of classic oratory. They do not demand you strike majestic ceremonial poses, hand raised high waving your papers with the other gripping your lapel as *Disraeli* did. The religious thundering pulpit tone of *Massillon* casting accusations of sin and warnings of fire and brimstone have similarly been confined to history. *Lincoln* in his still enshrined godhood among public speakers, whose usual speeches lasted two hours or more, would be chastised for their length today. (However, this may explain the impact of the two-minute Gettysburg address when others spoke for hours upon end – it was something new and an especially brave thing to do).

In short, whatever you plan to say, say it as you have practiced thus far. Ensure you be brave, be bold and be yourself; speak not *at* your audience, but *with* and *for* them.

HOW TO BUILD CHARISMA AND STAGE PRESENCE

Being a leader gives you charisma. If you look and study the leaders who have succeeded, that's where charisma comes from, from the leading.

SETH GODIN

You may believe charisma to be an inborn trait. This is untrue. Although a baby may be charming to its parents, a majority of others would find it practically revolting. People are only charismatic because they say what their listeners want to hear and show them what they want to be shown.

I loathe the notion that charisma is built by merely wearing well-fitting clothes, having a great smile and giving a strong handshake. All these elements help, but in the end, they are merely superficial. Much as no amount of layers of varnish atop an oak table will support rotten knots and burls which undermine the entire structure nor will vanities upon your person. You may be dressed in the most lavish levels of sartorial pride, have teeth as white as pearls and a perfectly measured handshake, but you may still quake when left alone with your thoughts if you lack self-confidence.

Charisma and poise must be carefully cultivated via an equal level of self-acceptance, humility and appreciation for the needs of others. Good-dress and adornment is necessary for a strong first impression, but no embellishment will support a weak personality devoid of sharing what an audience wishes to hear.

What then makes an impressive looking speaker? For one; if you wish to be perceived as a key person on a stage of several others find a way to subtly stand out. This may be being the only individual with a lapel microphone when others are using a handheld, it could be standing up to speak when addressing a particularly important question or being that rare gem who is able to effortlessly recite an allegorical story with humour, humility and insight which encapsulates your expertise. Similarly, when making a point on stage, stand still. When telling a story, roam (but don't go too far, because the lights might not be able to follow you). When ending a speech, know which side to leave. These techniques work, but much like spice added to a dish they should be measured precisely for a perfect balance. If you try these techniques do not attempt them all at once and steal the limelight, because this will leave you only to be seen as a boor by your peers and your audience - no one like those who interrupt or usurp others.

Yet, none of these suggestions truly foster charisma, they merely project it. Instead charisma is fostered by a number of complimentary parts which support each other.

Here are several suggestions to internalise that mystical magnetism:

CULTIVATE SELF-CONFIDENCE

Firstly, cultivate self-confidence by achieving goals which align with your values. Much as a tree will grow as tall as it can, twisting and pushing its way around hindrances, overturning rock and wire or internalising foreign obstacles into its thick bark if necessary; nothing preventing it from reaching as far as it can with the energy it has at its disposal, so too must a person who lacks self-confidence with the barriers which hinder their lives. Those lacking in confidence must strive with every fibre of their being to grow their self-worth, to improve their weaknesses and to overcome the vices which demean their true virtue by discovering what it is they wish to be confident at. No person is confident in every situation; that is a myth perpetrated by self-styled gurus with courses to sell. Instead, it is only continuous effort coupled with the repetition of micro-successes aligning with one's chief aim which will instil within one a sense of purpose and self-worth. It is nigh-on impossible to radiate personal warmth and self-acceptance if you fail to appreciate your own victories and hard-earned advantages - no matter how small they may be.

Be wary of surrounding yourself with friends or media which serves to demean your soul and belittle your mind. Ask yourself, what is the benefit in interreacting with that person, watching that show or reading that comment? I once had a career advisor who upon learning I had a memory disability said: *'you're best of being happy working at a factory, because you won't get far in life if you can't remember stuff'*. Such a person was of no value to my self-confidence and was swiftly removed from my social circle. Similarly, many have been tainted by friends who made them the butt of a joke, which like the smallest poison dripped slowly into the bloodstream can bring down the strongest beast.

If you do shrink your friend group do not retreat into perpetual isolation. This will only serve to give time for crippling introspection, because for many the scariest place is the be left alone with their own thoughts. Instead, mingle with the self-confident, study their mannerisms and let them enrich your mind with new ideas and purpose.

LEARN MORE AND THEN ACT

If you wish to grow your intellectual charisma then act on the obtaining of new knowledge. When you read a great book which inspires you, put the inspiring passages down into writing and practice what you have learned immediately; do not fall into the trap of seeking new knowledge. It is better to be a small-minded practitioner of the virtues of one book than a bookworm who has read ten and acted on none.

I have met many who have achieved little in comparison to their peers and yet hold themselves in healthier levels of esteem, because they do not compare themselves to others. Although these people are neither rich nor burdened with responsibilities, they hold themselves in well-mannered high regard. They do not demean themselves nor talk as if they have wasted their lives. They are content with their standing and are studiously working towards personal satisfaction. Regardless of income or status, these people still, like all of us, have problems which tug at their hearts and bring them into the depths of sorrow. Yet, they hold such pain tight towards their chest and refuse to let it define them. If they have weaknesses, it is shown to others as a problem to be overcome rather than one which has defeated them. Adopting this search for opportunities can be transformative.

GRATITUDE IS WORTH MORE THAN GOLD

Some believe a treasury of disposable income will bring confidence. Although it is a dream for many, experience has taught me it cannot be relied upon, for I have worked with clients whose incomes have eclipsed mine in magnitudes of scale one can scarcely believe, whose palatial houses contain every luxury, whose concierges can make calls which will meet every whim. Yet, these same self-made people tell me how they awaken each morning and sigh; feeling as if they are failures or frauds of the highest magnitude. It was only through genuine gratitude for hard-won achievements that their empowered personality emerged. Be humble in the company of others, but appreciate achievements honed by your own hands with those most empowering of words; *'I like myself'*.

LISTEN WELL

Second to having self-confidence, the charismatic listen and listen well, allowing them to connect on an emotional level to their audiences. They speak in a language which fills their audience's needs. Their genuine authenticity shows that they enjoy being with others. This is not to say all charismatic people are extroverted. Some of the most charismatic people I have met despise the company of crowds or the eyes of an audience. Yet, in their silence they spent the time to observe, consider and empathise with the needs of others, granting them the ability to connect in ways the boor never could. The charismatic type never interrupts, never one-up's another's story nor do they demean. They show that the opinions of others are worthwhile and even if they disagree, they do so in a way which shows that the input given to them was considered.

DON'T POISON THE WELL

Water drawn from a poisoned well has the ability to bring an entire village to its knees. So too does poison administered to your mind. Ted Bundy was supposedly charismatic to both his victims and his investigators, because he mimicked their personalities, he spoke in a calm manner and used repetitive rhetoric, all culminating in a chilling demonstration that when people hear what they desire to hear, they believe what they desire to believe. Yet, through his actions he was the epitome of a poisoned soul.

Clean hands, a clean soul and a clean mind will work wonders for your charisma. If you drink, practice sobriety. If you smoke, practice healthy living. If you are self-sabotaging your performance through vice, practice abstinence. You need not be a chaste monk, but you must become the captain of your soul and the commander of your willpower. If you are respectful in your thoughts, dignified in your manner and earnest in your words others will idolise you.

What you did yesterday has resulted in who you are today, what you do today will make you who you'll be tomorrow. Your practice will build your abilities. It is only self-limitation, self-sabotage and self-destruction of the mind and body which end with the most harrowing of words '...*what if?*'.

MANAGING SPEAKING ANXIETY

It's all right to have butterflies in your stomach. Just get them to fly in formation.

ROB GILBERT

The most common issue which stops people from speaking in public is anxiety. The word 'anxiety' comes from the Latin word '*angusta*' which may be translated as "*a narrowing space that presses down upon one*". Thus, speaking anxiety may be envisioned as the ego fearing it will be caved in upon until it is paralyzed, or crushed like in the constricting coils of an anaconda.

When we become scared or anxious, our bodies enter fight or flight. The brain stimulates the production of the hormones adrenalin and cortisol. The muscles tense, the breathing becomes shallow and we feel a sensation of cold in our stomach. Tunnel vision and dilated pupils follow making those attempting to read a script struggle even more, along with a dry mouth, making it harder to speak.

Yet, isn't it strange how all of these physiological symptoms appear in the moment of excitement? Before a thrill the heart races, the palms sweat, the eyes focus and butterflies flitter in the stomach.

There are numerous ways to combat anxiety and below are a mixture of psychological and physiological methods which myself and my clients have found to be particularly useful:

- Acknowledge fear as being a natural response, even famous actors or pop-stars feel the same as you!

- Reframe 'fear' as 'excitement', because both carry the same bodily responses.

- Realise there is no 'right way' to perform; you are not following a musical score and expected to say every word perfectly.

- If you find yourself shaking, use wider gestures and open body language.

- Using informal everyday language rather than complex terminology will lessen the burden on your brain and allow for a more natural, flowing style of speech rather than awkward pauses.

- If you are due to have an interview or meeting with the C-suite, present to their LinkedIn profile picture beforehand for practice.

- Remember also it is not 'you vs them', your audience are not the paparazzi waiting for you to slip-up.

- Pre-rehearsing your introduction will allow you to talk through the nerves and accommodate yourself in your new environment.

- Practice mindfulness. You cannot change a thought once you've had it or stop thinking, but you can choose to acknowledge bad ones, let them go and then be grateful for doing so.

- Are you a non-native speaker? We don't expect perfection from someone doing their best.

However, after exploring and applying these examples, if issues persist, consult the next section for a unique exercise I've devised to assist those in dire straits.

PAVLOV'S PERFUME

Mindfulness can be an extremely grand subject but on the other hand it's very basic, it is basically, memory.

JOSEPH SORENSEN

I am neither a psychologist nor a therapist, therefore this chapter does not constitute medical advice – but what I write of here has never failed me or my clients.

On rare occasions, I work with a client who is so utterly overwhelmed by fear that none of the previous strategies help to alleviate their anxiety. These are the people who dare not answer the phone, who shy from the microphone or fail to even show their face on a webcam. It can be challenging working with these people, but eventually seeing their faces and hearing their voices is especially rewarding.

You may question, how can someone who doesn't wish to speak have a voice lesson? I did too the first time I met one of these clients! Yet, I believe everyone has the capacity to speak and for the extremely anxious I created a technique which over time slowly dispels anxiety. I name the practice *'Pavlov's Perfume'*.

Ivan Pavlov (1849-1936) was a Russian physiologist known primarily for his work on *classical conditioning*. Classical conditioning is the ability to create a response in the mind and body upon receiving a particular stimulus. You may have conditioned yourself without knowing it. If you repeatedly check your phone for new updates without intending to, this is classical conditioning. If you associate a particular food with feeling as if you were at home, this is classical conditioning. When you associate a certain perfume or aftershave with public speaking, this will be classical conditioning.

In Pavlov's most famous experiment, he found that he could make a dog salivate by merely ringing a bell moments before feeding it. Eventually even when no food was presented, the dog would salivate on command at the ring of the bell.

Taking inspiration from Pavlov, I suggest to these highly anxious clients that they purchase a perfume or aftershave which was to be worn *only* during practice sessions and live speaking events. Applying the perfume during the lesson and then washing it off immediately afterwards is crucial, because the intention is to condition the olfactory senses to associate the perfumed scent with successful practice and positive feedback. The results were transformative. With enough exposure every individual demonstrated enormously increased confidence during speaking events when wearing the scent they had associated with successful practice.

If you intend to use *'Pavlov's Perfume'* in your own practice, I would suggest you place a heavy dab of the perfume on your hands and neck, which will cause the perfume to naturally waft upwards towards your nose as you speak. However, as a warning; if you are due to speak with someone in polite company, ensure your scent of choice is not overpowering.

Finally, it is especially important you apply it only during your practice and then wash it off immediately afterwards, because if you have a miserable day whilst wearing the perfume, you could ruin the association!

MANAGING STAGE FRIGHT

The best way to conquer stage fright is to know what you're talking about.

MICHAEL H. MESCON

Years ago, a private hedge-fund manager contacted me in a cold sweat. He had been suffering from nightmares after reading that the venue he was due to speak at had the capacity to hold 70,000 people; a gargantuan number far beyond the scope of his usual speeches to a handful of executives.

Asking for more details, he explained the talk was to centre around a product offering for extreme-net-worth clients and would be of little interest to the general public. His usual talks were delivered at his company boardroom on the lavishly decorated top floor to a small number of his familiar peers. Understandably, the idea of being thrust to the forefront from such a small stage to envisioning being before tens of thousands of eyes was gnawing at his confidence. Despite regularly managing portfolios worth billions of dollars, an unimaginable sum to myself, I will never forget him saying *"the idea of speaking to even 1/10,000[th] of that turns me into a gibbering mess"*.

Thinking about the situation I couldn't shake the feeling that something was wrong. Why would a lucrative investment firm hire a concert-hall sized venue for such a niche investment opportunity? Why would they suddenly take a hedge-fund manager and put him on the centre stage to talk to tens of thousands, rather than choosing a more experienced talker such as the CEO? I suspected a mistake had been made and suggested he make some inquiries.

A few days passed and then good news. I was right. After instructing him to clarify with the organisers the number of people *expected to attend,* he discovered that yes, the venue could hold 70,000 people, but only 12 had booked a seat. The envisioned grand stage turned out to be a small, discrete room which had been especially chosen for a particular VIP whose security entourage had deemed escaping from the top floor of a skyscraper in the event of an emergency to be a liability not worth taking.

This little incident demonstrates how even a minor misunderstanding can easily spiral out of control and cause stage fright which is, at its very core, *a fear of the unknown.*

Therefore, one of the best ways to manage stage fright is to obtain as much information as possible about the event. Doing so will allow you to give a stellar performance and it is an absolute necessity if you are a paid speaker.

Charles Osgood, the American radio-television commentator and writer once said that *"he who traces out the route up to the speaking place, avoids the all too common fate of falling on his face!"* J. R. R. Tolkien said *"...it does not do to leave a live dragon out of your calculations, if you live near him"* and although your audience is no *Smaug: King Under the Mountain*, knowing the answer to the following questions will lessen the burden when called to speak on a stage:

- When is the talk?

- Where is the talk?

- How long is your talk?

- What would make the organisers happy?

- What is the message you are expected to convey?

- What is the purpose of the audience attending?

- Has the audience been recently made redundant, lost a large sum of money or experienced a similar incident?

- What should you not mention?

- What is the average age of the audience?

- What is their level of experience?

- What is the makeup of your audience?

- Are there any dignitaries who should be thanked or introduced before you commence your talk?

- Does your audience use acronyms for particular phrases?

- Are there any terms or gestures which are normal to yourself but considered rude in this area?

- Are there any religious or political affiliations to include or avoid mentioning?

- How are the transport links to the venue if you are reliant upon a bus or train?

- Could you be late from detours or jostled by an uncomfortable ride?

- How is the accommodation if you are staying overnight?

- If you are speaking in a developing country is the food safe to eat and water safe to drink?

- What are the procedures in the event of an emergency?

- Will there be people speaking before you?

- Will you be introduced by an MC?

- If someone is speaking after you, are you expected to introduce them?

- Will you be speaking from a podium or lectern?

- Can I have the podium or lectern removed?

- Will you have a presentation clicker?

- When can I test the microphone in advance?

- If the microphone is battery powered, it is fully charged?

- How do I turn off the microphone so it doesn't relay any backstage conversations?

- What is the reverb like in the room?

- Will I need to bring my own laptop?

- Does my laptop have a neutral background?

- Is my laptop liable to crash when presenting?

- Who do I email my presentation slides to?

- Have I put my slides on a USB stick?

- How is the stage lighting?

- Can I see the entire audience from the stage?

- Will there be a blinding spotlight shining at me?

- If you're wearing new shoes, have you broken them in?

- Do you have a backup shirt to change into off-stage if the lights are sweltering for when you socialise afterwards?

- How many are expected to attend your talk?

- How are the audience seated?

- Will alcohol be served at the venue, leading to a potentially rowdy crowd?

- Will there be a Q&A?

- How long is the Q&A liable to last?

- Who manages the Q&A?

- Will there be a break during my talk?

- Can I use shots from this talk in my marketing material?

- Do I need to sign a non-disclosure agreement (NDA)?

- Are there liable to be potential hecklers or protestors?

- If so, why?

- Have you catered your talk to all these findings?

- When and how much do you get paid?

Once you have answered these questions, you may still hold some fear in your heart. This is normal and to be expected. However, it can be managed by rebranding some of the physiological symptoms as mentioned earlier. Often, a limiting mentality induces many of these physiological issues, therefore it is necessary to remind yourself *people are attending your talk because they want to hear what you have to say*. You will have something which clearly demonstrates your knowledge, your skill or your personality which others can benefit from.

Finally, remind yourself of your successes, your practice and developing skill in articulating your thoughts to become a master speaker – speaking on stage can be scary at first, but the rewards are worth the fright.

DEALING WITH HECKLERS

You can spend your time on stage pleasing the heckler in the back, or you can devote it to the audience that came to hear you perform.

SETH GODIN

By speaking in public, you are establishing yourself as an expert in your field – something which potentially no amount of other work may grant upon you. Although very few people attend a talk in hopes of seeing someone fail, there are those who, as Frank Sinatra crooned *'get their kicks stomping on a dream'*.

As you gain more attention you are liable (in rare cases) to attract people who believe they deserve their own share of your hard-earned attention, meaning you may meet with a heckler or protestor. If this happens, do not dismay. Your audience will be sympathetic to any interruptions both you and they face as things revert back to normal. The most important thing is to never lose your temper.

In my experience there are three kinds of heckler:

- *Passive* – those who merely refuse to stop talking amongst themselves whilst you are speaking.

- *Active* – often professional rabble-rousers, these are the people who intend on causing disruption to defame and undermine you or use your platform to further an unrelated cause.

- *Moral Crusader* – angry types who hijack speaking opportunities to satisfy a narcissistic need to further an (often ignorant) counter ideology which supports their fragile ego.

Should an interruption occur, first and foremost establish if the offending individual is actually a heckler. Not everyone who asks a difficult question is looking to defame you. Those who interrupt may not have an ulterior motive, they may simply lack social skills or have a poor understanding of your topic. In comparison, a heckler will usually begin by starting with an aggressive comment, shouting an insult or proposing a loaded question. *Ad hominin* insults will usually follow aimed at yourself, your organisation or your thoughts. Some may take to the stage uninvited with banners, flags or placards. In almost all instances, your audience will most likely drown out any complaints with boo's or demands for the interrupting individual(s) to be removed. Some may spray offending scents in the room, which in the most unfortunate instance may require for your talk to be either postponed or moved elsewhere. Such instances are as a whole, out of your control. The venue management will know what to do.

In my view given the nature of free speech it is important that despite a heckler not treating you with respect, you should treat them with respect. Allowing them the freedom to speak will show they are of little threat to you. This is not to say you should simply open your body to being assaulted; self-defence is more than permittable if necessary. Don't take it too far though. In an incident known as 'Rumble in Rhyl' the Labour MP *John Prescot*, an amateur boxer in his youth, once returned an egging with a significant punch to a street protestor. Prescot's natural response to seeing red may be defendable, but in the political realm it significantly tarnished his professional reputation. Compare this to *Arnold Schwarzenegger* and *George Bush* calmly responding to being on the receiving end of a shoe, as if nothing had happened.

For *passive* hecklers, it is always best to continue talking. If you pause and wait for them to quieten down, you may appear weak and servile. When speaking in public you are perceived as an expert authority on your topic; waiting for others to be quiet does not project authority. If the interruption does continue, it may be advisable to make a stern yet polite request for conversation to be made outside of the venue. In this instance address the audience rather than the offending individual, because making eye contact with the passive heckler has the potential to lead to a more serious interruption. If you are presenting online, the global mute button is your friend.

If your talk is interrupted by an *active* heckler who is either aggressive or intending on drowning out your speech, it is best to wait for the security to remove them from the premises. This may take a substantial amount of time, dependant on the venue, staff and the actions of the protestors – who often have an annoying habit of chaining themselves to immovable objects.

I would strongly advise you do not attempt to be funny or provide a witty repartee to a heckler, because this is the attention they are craving. Engaging with them will drag you down to their level, which often results with them beating you with experience. Some hecklers are professional rabble-rousers who relish in making personal attacks. No matter how cutting these may be, avoid eye contact with the heckler and if necessary address the audience with undeniable facts to counter their claim.

Moral Crusaders honestly believe themselves to be doing something good and virtuous. These are usually those who whilst at college or university could not submit an essay on time, yet believe they could rule the world. Poorly socialised, their beliefs are so ideologically ingrained into their emotions that all rational thought has been usurped. Failing to look inwards at their own inadequacies, they instead have immersed themselves in radical, resentful echo-chambers masquerading as circles of empowerment, all which boost their fragile ego. Depending on their political beliefs, be it far-left or far-right, these people will never see any merits to your words, because they have been brainwashed to see you as 'the enemy'. In their minds, they and they alone have the moral superiority and you are either with them, or against them. In their protests expect them to scream, stomp and act like spoiled children. Engaging with these hecklers is futile. You are best to wait in confident silence, minding your body language until security have them removed. On rare occasions it can be favourable to speak about the damage such a mindset holds to society at large – if you feel comfortable enough to do so.

To calm your emotional state during a heckling, an excellent exercise is box breathing. This is the act of inhaling for four seconds, holding for four seconds and then exhaling for four seconds. During your silent calming exercise, the audience's annoyance will most likely speak louder than you ever could. Once a protestor has been removed try not to reference the interruption again, because this will only detract from your authority as an expert in your industry.

Finally, in almost all instances when a protester leaves or is escorted out by security, audiences may clap and cheer. This usually works in your favour, because it allows for a stronger emotional bonding between yourself and the audience, but jeering should not be encouraged. Instead, always publicly thank the security staff for their hard work, because they are likely to be on the receiving end of up-close and personal abuse outside of the venue even after your talk has ended.

WHAT ABOUT STAGE EQUIPMENT?

Failure to prepare is preparing to fail.

Assuming your speech has been prepared and the venue hired, it is always advisable to ensure certain specific equipment will be made available. Unfortunately, many venues will lie and fail to provide the necessary equipment unless you obtain a promise of provision in writing. In most instances, you will have an events-organiser at hand. However, here are a few suggestions of thing to double check.

Whenever possible, always opt for a lapel (lavalier) microphone over a handheld one. A handheld microphone can become heavy after just a few minutes. You don't want to be exhausted halfway through your speech. Second, a lavalier is unobtrusive, whereas a handheld microphone robs you of half your body language. You can't gesture naturally if you have a hand stuck beneath your chin. You may have the choice of a lavalier which is clipped to your clothing or worn around your face. I would suggest you choose the clothing option as these are less intrusive. Some sound engineers prefer to clip the microphone to your lapel whilst others prefer to tie it into your tie to hide it. Consider also your body language. If you grab your lapels or have a habit of being expressive with your arms, it is possible to accidentally brush against it creating a harsh noise. You can test to see if this will be an issue by purchasing a comically large broach and wearing it on your lapel in private practice.

Second, if you are to be using slides, ensure the venue has an ability to display them in a professional manner. Vintage overhead projectors with plastic screens which need to be manually positioned will undermine your professionalism. Take three copies of your digital slides; one on a memory stick and email the other to yourself and the venue organisers for display. Check also if you need to bring your own laptop and purchase a selection of display-port adaptors.

It is worth noting that stage lighting can be blinding. I have had several clients express to me how upon walking onstage they are dazzled by lights and unable to see the audience. If that happens, continue to scan across the horizon as if you could see the audience perfectly. Also remember to wear a generous amount of perspiration-preventing deodorant; the brighter the lights the more intense the heat. It can often reach over 30°C / 86°F on even a small stage.

If you have chosen to speak with a podium, ensure beforehand it's not too tall. I remember once a client told me an embarrassing story of giving a speech in Sweden where the average male height is 5'11", over seven inches taller than he was - leaving him almost unable to be seen behind the oversized podium. If the podium is too tall, ask for either a booster or steps. If neither of these are available forgo the podium if possible.

One problem particularly nervous speakers face is accidentally rushing past their slides. This can often come across as unprofessional when you try to update them in rapid succession. A simple method of avoiding this is to practice using a presentation remote by using either a dog training clicker, which produces a loud *click* when pressed, or by holding a pen and similarly clicking it when you intend to move to a new slide. This will act as an audible reinforcement to your subconscious to save you playing catch-up with your slides.

CHAPTER 7

IDENTIFYING DETRIMENTAL SPEECH HABITS

It took me quite a long time to develop a voice, and now that I have it, I am not going to be silent.

MADELEINE ALBRIGHT

Outlined in earlier chapters was a stress on the importance of identifying how you speak. Usual weaknesses include: beginning a sentence with '*so*', ending a sentence with '*so, urr, yea*', or misusing a common phrase. These were all linguistic errors. Much as it would be distracting to read this book if the type was not set correctly, the same inconvenience is felt by your listener for similar omissions in your speech. Therefore, the following section adapted from my previous work '*Speak and Be Heard: 101 Vocal Exercises for Voice Actors, Public Speakers and Professionals*' (2019) will serve as an excellent guide to identifying any poor mechanical, tonal or generally detrimental speech habits which could be diminishing your spoken abilities.

It is possible to become overwhelmed and dejected given the intense scrutiny you are now paying towards your articulation skills. I have known a small number of students to express how ignorance of such matters would have been far more pleasant. I would therefore strongly recommend to be on your guard for any negative ruminations concerning how you think or speak. It is not necessary for you to reach perfection, nor is it possible. Instead, you should merely attempt to identify if it is possible for you to learn from a recent conversation with either yourself or another individual. If something can be learned, ensure you write it down in well-defined terms to aid with your improvement.

Consulting the following pages may further help with identifying any other poor habits you may not have considered:

THE MONOTONE SPEAKER

Nothing is more stale to a listener than a monotone voice completely devoid of life and musical character. Every statement the monotonous speaker makes is seemingly an utterance of disinterest and indifference. A monotone nature is often found by those who are unable to impart emotion towards what they are reading rather than a neurological affliction; the truly monotonous speaker could confess the words *'I love you'* and spitefully state *'I despise you'* with an equally unenthusiastic nature.

SOLUTION

Sing when you speak! Imagine your words are on an impossible staircase, with each word dropping down and then stepping back up to differing pitches. Take it to the extreme.

Consider also how the tonality of your voice could be interpreted by your listeners. Consider ending each phrase on an upward or downwards inflection, depending on whether you are making a statement or asking a question.

Perhaps create a change in speed and pitch. Try rushing and adding a higher pitch for moment of excitement or slowing down and dropping your voice to a lower tone for when you truly wish to capture your audience's attention.

Once you are comfortable with this exercise, be careful not to overemphasise your tonality lest you sound like a radio announcer with a predictable musical cadence.

THE DEJECTED EEYORE

I am sure that at least one point in life you have come across a long-suffering individual who has a voice so mired by disappointment that they have an almost uncanny ability to bring everyone around them down to their miserable level. These are the people for who enthusiasm seems to have been replaced by a complete and utter shell of self-pity and misery. Perhaps this is the result of misfortune, or more seriously poor mental health. The Eeyore's voice often sinks to the lower tones and slurs lethargically from one word to another, only to raise ever so slightly upon a moment of surprise, immediately to be shot down.

SOLUTION

Seeking professional help may be the first course of action as mental health issues may be the cause that no amount of positive thinking or mindfulness may solve.

For others, this voice is purely reflective of their philosophical mindset and cannot be changed through simple vocal tutoring. If this is not the case yet you still struggle, you should start with attempts to mimic the rapid-fire delivery of professional motivational speakers such as *Les Brown*, *Zig Ziglar* and *Tony Robbins*.

Furthermore, experiment with raising the tone of your voice and deliver your words in a staccato nature. Consulting the previous section on 'how to express emotion' would also be beneficial.

YES, I CAN HEAR YOU!

In 1950's, the US army attempted to discover the ideal volume to issue orders to cadets. Their experiments found soldiers were often incapable of replying to an order at a different volume than they were spoken to. If shouted at, the soldiers shouted back and if whispered at, they whispered in response. Unfortunately, we all know someone who lacks an 'indoor voice', the Sergeant Major with a gruff, overbearing tone which would be more suited to barking gravelly orders to soldiers rather than delivering a quiet eulogy. These people don't realise their speaking volume is set at high levels. If you notice you tend to have a personal space almost twice as wide as those around you and your personal hygiene isn't suspect, your listeners may have retreated to protect their eardrums.

SOLUTION

Overbearing speakers often do not realize the volume they are producing is painful to their listeners. The constant high volume can also be interpreted as anger or an unapproachable nature. Many feel as if they are being spoken 'at' rather than spoken 'to'. If you have found you are often being informed your voice is too loud, practice whispering and reducing the volume at which you speak. You may also want to have your hearing checked, because often those who speak too loud have undiagnosed hearing issues. Do not be worried you are speaking too quietly in public, for if this is the case people are far more likely to ask you to speak up than to be quiet.

OH SORRY, I SAID-

These are the words of the especially weak-voiced speaker. Constantly repeating themselves, they spend half their speaking lives in a perpetual loop of reiterating something which if said clearly in the first place, would lead them onto the next topic. Weak voices are nothing to be ashamed of, however. Studies have found quieter people are often from upbringings which experienced strict rules or were subject to punishment for stating their opinion. If this is the case, your actions may be the result of past emotional distress especially if as a child you were told to be 'seen and not heard'. Therapy may help with this, but for now attempt the solution below.

SOLUTION

A weak voice is hindered by a lack of support from the diaphragm while speaking. If you find people are often asking you to speak up and repeat what you are saying consider investing some time in cardio exercise.

To improve you need to first ensure each sentence begins with a full breath which can allow you to project your voice across a room. Secondly, ensure when speaking you speak towards your listener's ears, not towards their feet. It may make you feel uncomfortable to speak loudly at first, but by consistent practice your confidence will grow with every word, resulting in a stronger voice and more interest from your listeners.

THE VENTRILOQUIST

There are some people whose lips are so tightly pursed when speaking, we barely see the whites of their teeth. Others have a habit of speaking out of only one side of their mouth. Often, every sound which manages to escape this vocal prison is a mumbled mess, but once again this can be improved through practice.

SOLUTION

Observe yourself in a mirror; do you talk with an open mouth or are your lips brought tightly together?

Do your words form with a lilt, your mouth being drawn towards the left or right side of your face?

Do you talk with only your bottom lip, by forcing your top lip against your teeth?

If you do notice any of these symptoms, pucker your lips as if you were to make an exaggerated kiss, ensuring you are facing directly towards the mirror. Then, attempt to talk. Although this does look rather silly, it will force the muscles previously ignored into action. Once you feel a fluidity of movement returning, slowly bring your lips back and ensure you form each word with an over enunciated movement. Repeat this every day for ten minutes until you notice an improvement.

THE DRUNK SOUNDALIKE

We all know of one person who sounds as if they have drunk a little too much when speaking. Unfortunately, slurred words are a common hindrance to clear speech, especially when the sounds become an agglutination into one amorphous group.

"Ifyoutaykea 'ook ove'rere, you'llbeableto seea' talltawaa..."
(If you take a look over there, you'll be able to see a tall tower...)

SOLUTION

Care must first be taken to identify which particular sounds, words of phrases are often joined together. Ask a friend to point out when you are slurring your words or record yourself and listen to any phrases which sound garbled.

To improve, ensure you add a brief pause to emphasise the gaps between each word or check the speed of your speech. Practice the previously mentioned exercise on adding a staccato nature to your words, making the sounds crisp and clear.

Also remember not all who slur are speaking too slowly. Some slur because they speak too quickly. If this is the case, focus on emphasising your words.

THE PAINED SPEAKER

Some speakers find they are unable to talk for short periods of time without going red in the face or they lose their voices after speaking for extended periods of time. Yet, why is it a baby can scream for hours on end without fatigue? The reason is a baby has yet to learn poor techniques of breath support or is engaging in conscious vocal restraint.

SOLUTION

To guarantee you can speak for long periods, you need to ensure you are using *diaphragmatic breaths* rather than *chest breaths*.

Firstly, let's illustrate a poor breathing technique: take a deep breath and then suck in your stomach. This is a *chest breath* and is it especially difficult to talk in this manner. A chest also breath places great strain upon the vocal cords due to the limited amount of air available.

Now, take a deep breath but allow your stomach to fall naturally outwards. Your shoulders should rise ever so-slightly if you do this correctly. This is a *diaphragmatic breath* and is the style you will naturally learn to adopt with practice.

Once you have corrected your breathing, another tip once recommended in antiquity was to 'speak on the end of a yawn'. This is as simple as it sounds; practice vocalising a yawn and when you feel your voice is most relaxed, continue to speak. You will eventually feel your voice is almost incapable of being strained as you are no longer forcing your volume or tensing the muscles in your throat. If you struggle with this exercise due to tension, attempt to add a silent 'h' to the beginning of certain words, such as the old American accent which vocalised a silent h in words such as '(h)when' or '(h)Wednesday'. This is especially important for strong words which utilise a glottal attack, such as 'at' 'and' and the movie directors' favourite: 'action!'

THE NASAL SPEAKER

Have you ever heard someone who sounds similar to a train conductor speaking over a loudspeaker which lacks a rich warmth or depth? This is a 'nasal' voice and is caused by the air in the speaker's voice being expelled through their nose rather than their mouth. Nasal voices often have two qualities, either shrill or weak dependent on the pitch of the voice. Male nasal voices are often considered as juvenile or effeminate and conjure images of *Pee-wee Herman*. Whereas female nasal voices are often considered as shrill due to the ear-splitting frequencies they produce, especially if the owner has a strong set of lungs behind them such as the actress *Fran Drescher*. Frankly, it is impossible to have a warm and sonorous nasal voice as there simply isn't enough resonance in the nasal cavity to produce pleasant tones.

SOLUTION

Hold your nose and read this paragraph out loud, but rather than pushing your voice towards your nasal cavity try and make all the air exit your mouth. (Note: this will not be possible with words which utilize the nasal cavity to form, such as closed mouthed 'm' and 'p' sounds). Once you can ascertain the difference between your nasal and spoken voice, release your fingers from your nose and speak naturally.

THE 'MASK' SPEAKER

There is much debate amongst voice and acting tutors as to the benefit or detriment of 'speaking from the mask'. You can find the 'mask' by humming *'mmm'* until you feel the area between your nose and lips (named the philtrum) beginning to vibrate, rather than your chest. At this point, you will notice if you shift your voice from the back of your throat to the mask by lowering and rising your larynx the pitch will increase due to a lack of resonance in the mouth. It is my view, speaking from the mask can be a hindrance to both breath control and pleasant speech, as it is reliant on nasal speaking and should therefore be avoided.

SOLUTION

Speaking from the mask is often caused by forcing the larynx to rise in the throat and adopting a nasal voice (as explained on the previous page). Mask speaking can be the result of stress, a forced high pitch or a lack of breath support. To prevent yourself from speaking from the 'mask' it is vital you relax the muscles in your larynx, neck and throat. First, place a hand upon your neck and feel exactly where your voicebox is in your throat and hum *'mmm'*. Then, slowly lower the tone of your voice until you feel your chest vibrate; this is your 'relaxed' state. Experiment until your voice naturally sits in this relaxed area.

THE GLOTTAL ATTACKER

Does your voice ever crack or pop when you say a series of short words in quick succession? This is due to a building of pressure behind the vocal cords and is often referred to as a 'glottal attack'. The words 'at', 'cat' and 'tat' are excellent examples of potential glottal attack words. Attempt to say them in a quick, staccato manner and feel for the pressure behind your vocal cords on the 'a' sound causing your larynx to jump. Now imagine what damage this jumping and cracking could do to your voice on a daily basis with the many thousands of times it is repeated! Recent studies have shown it only takes two minutes of incorrect glottal speech to cause the vocal cords to redden due to bruising. Therefore, you must be wary of how glottal attacks can damage your voice.

SOLUTION

As previously mentioned under the section concerning 'strained' speakers, affecting a breathy voice or silent 'h' to the beginning of glottal words is a beneficial way of training yourself out of these bad habits. Certain sounds, such as the 'm' in 'mother' do not produce a glottal attack therefore it would be beneficial for you to attempt to say the words 'mother cat' until you can identify the difference between a soft sound and a glottal attack.

THE CONTORTIONIST

A trait often found in thespians is the exaggerated movement of the mouth and lips when reciting their lines. On stage, this is often mandatory as their expressions needs to be visible at the back of an auditorium. However, in everyday life some speakers have the habit of speaking only from one side of the mouth, perhaps due to a childhood paradigm stemming from stress, stuttering or a similar muscular issue. If you find you are speaking from one side of your mouth by tugging your cheeks, you will struggle to enunciate your words clearly. Thankfully, this issue can be addressed, but remember even the most professional of speakers won't be able to mirror each side of their lips when they speak.

SOLUTION

Look at yourself in the mirror and question as to exactly why you speak from one side of your face. Is it a learned habit which can be unlearned or a matter of weakened muscles which can be trained? For both maladies, it would be best to begin to over-enunciate words slowly and meticulously when practising to build muscle tone and eradicate past habits.

A simple exercise would be to methodically repeat the vowel sounds 'A E I O U' in a slow and steady manner. Do this for two minutes every day, as often as possible until you notice a more balanced and natural movement of the lips.

If the unbalance is especially prominent, one particularly useful tool to consider purchasing is a *'Facial-flex'* which was originally developed to help stroke-recovering speakers rebuild muscle strength in the lips, cheeks and jaw.

THE UNNATURALLY PITCHED

I am sure you have heard someone who is noticeably forcing the pitch of their voice to either artificially high or low levels. Not only does this sound unnatural but it is also potentially damaging to the vocal cords. Just as any muscle should never be constantly tensed, the vocal cords also require moments of rest and relaxation. By artificially changing the pitch of your voice you are not only unconvincing, but you are also liable to develop painful and damaging vocal polyps which can only be removed via invasive surgery. This trait is commonly found amongst teenage boys who wish to sound more mature than their voices would suggest and women who are affecting a faux-feminine tone. Nature never intended you to force your voice box to move up or down when you speak, therefore you should relax and speak at a normal tone. However, if you have been forcing your voice to an altered pitch for a long period of time, you may have forgotten your natural tone. Try the solution below to help regain control of your natural voice.

SOLUTION

Imagine you were agreeing with someone by humming or saying the words '*uh-huh*'. The '*uh*' is often vocalised at the lowest relaxed pitch you can produce without any extra effort, whereas the '*huh*' is placed at just above your natural speaking pitch. Repeat the '*uh-huh*' phrase several times, ensuring you do not artificially change the pitch of your voice. You should eventually establish a natural speaking pitch just below the '*huh*' part of this exercise.

THE IRON JAW

If you wanted to better hear a conversation in another room, you wouldn't listen through the keyhole - you would open the door. Much the same could be said about speaking. To properly enunciate your words, a freedom of movement must be allowed to the jaw. Occasionally this is a hindrance to individuals conscious of their teeth or a similar personal matter. Therefore, this can also be an experiment in building confidence.

SOLUTION

If you find you rarely part your teeth when speaking, remember how clear diction is reliant on a natural freedom of the mouth. By consciously choosing to speak with a clenched mouth or solid jaw, you are hindering not only your diction but also the expression of emotion capable.

To begin with, allow the jaw to drop and then open the mouth as if comedically surprised. Hold the expression for five seconds and then return to a gently closed mouth. Repeating this several times along with gently sliding the jaw from side to side will be beneficial in releasing tension.

It is not unusual to hear some cracks and pops when first attempting this exercise, but as with all efforts there should never be any pain or discomfort.

If you are struggling, you should also practice the exercise on loosening the jaw using the words 'OO – OH – AH' for a few minutes, several times a day.

LISPS

As someone who was mocked for many years due to having a prominent lisp as a child, I can sympathise with others afflicted by this condition. A lisp may be a matter of a lack of muscular control which is allowing the tongue to protrude past the teeth when speaking. In especially rare cases it may be the tongue is too large for the mouth and therefore a specialist should be consulted as little muscular training can alleviate this. A lisp can also manifest in old age due to a fattening of the tongue thanks to a lack of communication and general muscle degradation. This is unfortunately prominent amongst those who live isolated lives.

SOLUTION

To alleviate a lisp, you first need to determine where you place your tongue when making an 's' sound. If your tongue is placed behind the bottom teeth, it needs to be arched upwards with the tip placed on gum-line behind the top front teeth (the alveolar ridge).

Try to avoid splaying the air out from either side of the top teeth, as this turns a crisp sound into mushy sound. You also want to avoid placing too much pressure on the gum line with the tip of your tongue. One student tried to imagine they were gently rolling an air bubble between their tongue and alveolar ridge which produced an immediate improvement.

In some instances, the tongue must be restrained back into the mouth when speaking rather than being allowed to protrude past the teeth (with the exception of producing the 'th' sound).

For closed mouth exercises, imagine you were rolling a boiled sweet inside your mouth or attempting to tie a knot in a piece of string using your tongue. For open mouth exercises, stick the tongue out to the far left, far right or flap it back and forth in private company!

THE PERFECTIONIST

Richard Burton has often been acclaimed as being the finest speaker of the English language in modern history. His mellifluous baritone pitch and near-perfect enunciation graced the ears of millions across the world. His vocal routine involved climbing mountains whilst reciting poem and verse to his mentor, who would slowly walk away from him whilst still demanding vocal clarity. Yet even Burton, a master of his trade, was known to occasionally fib lines or trip over his tongue; you can hear this for yourself by listening to the narration outtakes of *Jeff Wayne's 'War of the Worlds'* album. There are many speakers who are crippled by the worry of mispronouncing their words. Some hesitate to say anything and others even stutter when approaching trigger words. If you hope to never mispronounce a word again then you will be disappointed, such is the fickle nature of the detachment between the voice and the brain.

SOLUTION

Accept that both the brain and your voice are not infallible. No matter how much you practice you will still make mistakes. In fact, it is probably those very moments when you wish to quit practicing that you are making the most progress. At first, you will struggle with these exercises as you are placing a majority of your focus on correcting whatever problems you have. At this point you have yet to learn the automatic, subconscious control over your vocal abilities. However, with each word will come improvement, clarity and an eventual subconscious reinforcement.

THE 'MACHINE GUN' SPEAKER

Have you ever heard a person who speaks so quickly every word they say begins to blend into one?

Ifweweretowriteastheyspokeitwouldlooklikethis
(*If we were to write as they spoke it would look like this*)

SOLUTION

When speaking, a pause is often one of your most powerful tools; it is akin to a vocal comma or bold emphasis. Fast speech often leads to a lack of clarity and a weakness of the voice, it also can suggest to your listeners you are nervous or even worse, untrustworthy. Adding pauses between your words both aids enunciation and enables you to bring about dramatic effect to what is being said. It also enables the listener to consider what is being said and to contemplate on the situation and form a useful opinion, rather than an off the cuff remark.

If you find people are asking you to slow down, or to repeat what you are speaking; record yourself for 60 seconds and count the total number of words you said. Research has shown how sad, serious or complex conversations are ideally between 60 to 110 words per minute (wpm). Descriptive, instructional and statements of fact should average 125 wpm. Daily conversation should average no more than 164 wpm. Of course, the more pauses added, the slower the speech will be. Taming the speed of your speech can be difficult to do, but it can often be achieved by repeating your key point internally in your mind at the end of a phrase. Although it may seem worrying that you are speaking too slowly, you will eventually find speaking at around

130 wpm leads to more engaging conversations and greater clarity of thought.

SO URR... YEA, YOU KNOW WHAT I MEAN, LIKE?

One of the most common detrimental speech habits I hear are the words *'so urr... yea, you know what I mean like?'*.

Examining this phrase shows that the speaker is actually hoping for validation, because they are subconsciously attempting to explain their statement to themselves, rather than to their listener. When they make their statement, they are often unsure what they said is correct, not because they are worried it has been miscommunicated, but because they lack faith in the thoughts they have articulated.

SOLUTION

To avoid saying this phrase you must become a *'straight line talker'*. Buddhist monks are some of the greatest straight-line talkers, because they have spent thousands of hours in meditation eliminating extraneous thoughts. Similarly, religious ordainment ceremonies are mostly tests to see if they can communicate on highly complex topics without deviating from a singular line of thought. If they are unsure of how to answer a question, they will instead tell a story which is open to wider interpretation by the listener.

However, not everyone has the opportunity to become enlightened in their lifetime. Therefore, if you do utter the offending phrase, try to either follow the phrase with a further explanation of your thoughts or present the listener with a suitable allegorical story which allows for interpretation.

A SELECTION OF PHRASES

There is no such thing as presentation talent, it is called presentation skills.

DAVID J.P. PHILLIPS

This will be a contentious chapter, because I am suggesting you consider to adopt what may be deemed by some as 'flowery language' when simple language will suffice. Thankfully, as you develop your speaking skills, you will eventually come to rely upon a selection of well-rehearsed statements, quotes or phrases which support your assertations of which you should document. However, the memorisation of a small number of these statements may give you the inspiration you need to state a particular point, the opportune time to collect your thoughts and begin with an end in mind or the rope to cling to rather than fall into a pit of an awkward silence.

The following tried and tested expressions will therefore serve you well for exercises in composition, memorisation and contemplation.

ASSERTATIONS:

All this, I know well enough because...
All that is quite true...
All this is unnatural, because...
And, finally, have not these suggestions shown that...
And such, I say, is...
And the whole point of these observations is...
At first it does seem as though...
At this very moment, there are...
But it should still be argued that...
But let it be understood that...
But let us suppose all these...
But now, I repeat...
Enough has been said of...
Everybody has to say that...
Few people will dispute...
For this simple reason...
Hence, I repeat, it is...
Hence it is that...
I acknowledge the force of...
I allude to...
I am expecting to hear next...
I am going to suggest...
I am justified in regarding...
I am myself of opinion that...
I am naturally led on to speak of...
I am no friend to...

I am not arguing the...
I am not complaining of...
I am not denying that...
I am not disposed to deny...
I am not here to defend the...
I am not justifying the...
I am not speaking of exceptions...
I am not trying to absolve...
I am obliged to mention...
I am perfectly confident that...
I am persuaded that...
I am quite certain that...
I am sure, at least, that...
I assume that the argument for...
I assume, then, that...
I beg to assure you...
I believe in it as firmly as...
I believe you feel, as I feel, that...
I cannot but feel that...
I cannot do better than...
I cannot even imagine why...
I cannot, therefore, agree with...
I cannot very well...
I conclude that it was...
I do not absolutely assert...
I do not believe that...
I do not contend that...
I do not know on what pretence...
I do not mean to propose...
I do not mean to say...
I do not think it unfair reasoning to...
I entirely agree upon this point...
I firmly believe that...

I have already said, and I repeat it...
I have already alluded to...
I have always argued that...
I have no doubt that it is...
I have only to add that...
I have the strongest reason for...
I hope I have now made it clear that...
I know well the sentiments of...
I marvel that...
I may say further that...
I may take it for granted...
I mention them merely...
I merely indicate...
I myself feel confident...
I only wish to recognize...
I really cannot think it necessary to...
I reply with confidence that...
I rest my opinion on...
I see no reason to doubt...
I suppose most will recollect...
I think I am right in saying...
I think I can demonstrate that...
I think it our duty...
I think it well not to be disputed that...
I think that this is a great mistake...
I think these facts show that...
I venture to say...
I venture to think...
I will suppose the objection urged...
I would not be understood as saying...
If you wish the most conclusive proof...
In the light of these things...
In this point of view, doubtless...

It can scarcely be imagined that...
It cannot be too often repeated...
It certainly follows, then...
It does not appear to me...
It has been more than hinted that...
It is amazing that there are any among us...
It is difficult to conceive that...
It is exceedingly unlikely that...
It is in effect the reply of...
It is in quite another kind, however...
It is no more than fitting that...
It is not a good thing to see...
It is not a wise thing to...
It is not chiefly, however...
It is not surprizing that...
It is not to be denied that...
It is not wonderful that...
It is of little consequence...
It is singular that...
It is the most extraordinary thing that...
It looks to me to be...
It may in a measure be true that...
It seems a truism to say...
It was foolish to talk of...
It was rash to say...
It would be misleading to say...
It would be no less impracticable to...
It would be vain to seek...
It would do no good to repeat...
It would seem that...
Largely, I have no doubt, it is due...
Moreover, I am sure...
Moreover, I believe that...

My answer is, that...
My belief is that...
My own opinion is...
Next, I give you the opinion of...
No one realises this more...
No one will, with justice, say...
No one would take the pains to challenge the...
Nor am I, believe me, so arrogant as...
Nor can we imagine that...
Nor is this surprising...
Not many words are required to show...
Of course, it will be said that...
Of no less importance is...
On the whole, then, I observe...
Our position is unquestionable...
Perhaps the reason of this may be...
Something of extravagance there may be in...
Such is steadfastly my opinion that...
Surely, this is good and clear reasoning...
The conclusion is irresistible...
There is a cynicism which...
There is another sense in which...
There is much force in...
There is no danger of our overrating the...
There is no good reason why...
There is something suggestive in...
This being the case, you will see...
This is a great mistake...
This is the only remaining alternative...
Though all this is obvious...
To my own mind...
To this there can be but one answer...
We have no right to say...

We laugh to scorn the idea...
We may have an overpowering sense of...
We may rest assured that...
When all has been said, there remains...
When it can be shown that...
When that is said, all is said...
When we contemplate the...
When we reflect on these sentiments...
Where there is prejudice, it is no use to argue...
You and I may hold that...
You cannot assert that...
You cannot say that...
You know as well as I do...
You will say that...

OBJECTIONS:

A further objection to...
Again, can we doubt...
Alas! how often...
Believe me, it is quite impossible for...
Heaven forbid...
Here it will be objected to me...
I beg respectfully to differ from...
I differ very much from...
I have another objection to...
I think it impossible that...
I think, on the contrary, that...
My antagonism is only aroused when...
No, no...
Not quite so...
So much for...

Surely it is preposterous...
The audacity of the statement is...
The charge is false...
These absurd pretensions...
We cannot leave unchallenged the...
We deny it...
You may object at once, and say...
You may object that...

SENTENCE CONTINUATIONS:

Again, we have abundant instances...
All we do know is that...
And, again, it is to be presumed that...
Amid so much that is uncertain...
And, further, all that I have said...
And hence it continually happens...
And hence it is that...
And if I know anything of...
And I sometimes imagine that...
And I wish also to say that...
And just here we touch the vital point in...
And now it begins to be apparent...
And now we are naturally brought on to...
And pursuing the subject...
And so, in like manner...
And strange to say...
As far as my experience goes...
But all is not done...
But do not tell me that...
But I am not quite sure that...
But I will not dwell on...

But I will not pause to point out...
But in any case...
But I shall go still farther...
But it is fitting I should say...
But my idea of it is...
But somehow all is changed...
But to go still further...
But we have faith that...
I come, then, to this...
In a broader and a larger sense...
In order to carry out...
In the first place...
In the first place, then, I say...
In the first place there is...
In this respect they are...
In what I have to say...
It is not, however...
It was not so...
No matter what...
No wonder, then, that...
Nor, lastly, does this...
Nothing less...
Now, after what I have said...
On the contrary...
On the one hand...
On the other hand...
Since you have suffered me to...
So far is clear, but...
Surely, then...
Then, finally...
Thus, you see...
To this, likewise, it may be added...
With possibly a single exception...

With regard to what has been stated...
Yet it is plain...
Yet, strange to say...

STATEMENTS OF FACT:

And, in fact, it is...
And it is certainly true...
And now we are told...
And so again on that day...
And the same is true of...
And this is manifestly true...
As it were...
At times we hear it said...
But by no kind of calculation can we...
But further still...
But I digress...
But I recollect that...
But if you look seriously at facts...
But in fact, there is no reason for...
But waiving this assumption...
For instance, there surely is...
Fortunately, I am not obliged...
From time to time...
Happily, for us...
Hence, too, it has often, been said...
History is replete with...
I am aware that...
I am in sympathy with...
I am mainly concerned with...
I am not going to attempt to...
I am not insensible of...

I am told that the reason...

I am well aware that...

I believe in the...

I cannot believe it...

I can scarcely conceive anything...

I carry with me no hostile remembrance...

I come now to observe...

I do not forget that...

I do not mistrust the future...

I do not overlook the fact that...

I do not question this...

I do not vouch for...

I do not want to argue the question of...

I do not yield to any one...

I have all along been showing...

I have a right to think that...

I have heard it said recently...

I have indicted...

I have listened with pleasure to...

I have never been able to understand...

I have never fancied that...

I have no confidence, then, in...

I have no desire in this instance...

I have read of the...

I have said that...

I have spoken of...

I know that there is a difference of...

I read but recently a story...

I recollect that...

I remember once when...

I said just now...

I see no objection to...

I shall not undertake...

I use the word advisedly...
I was astonished to learn...
I was very much struck with...
I will answer, not by retort, but by...
I would not, indeed, say a word to extenuate...
If such is the fact, then...
In saying all this, I do not forget...
In view of these facts, I say...
It is but too true that...
It has been maintained that...
It has been said and said truly...
It has sometimes been remarked that...
It is a common observation that...
It is a curious fact that...
It is a fact to any one that...
It is a melancholy fact that...
It is a notorious fact that...
It is a thing commonly said that...
It is a very serious matter...
It is an undeniable truth that...
It is apparent that...
It is certain that...
It is certainly not sufficient to say...
It is historically certain that...
It is, indeed, commonly said...
It is more difficult to...
It is not alleged...
It is not long since I had occasion...
It is not proposed to...
It is not true that...
It is observable enough...
It is quite true that...
It is true, indeed, that...

It is well known that...

It need hardly be said that...

It seems now to be generally admitted...

It should also be remembered that...

It should be remembered...

It so happens that...

It was under these circumstances...

It will be easy to cite...

It will be found, in the second place...

It will be observed also that...

It will be well to recall...

It will not surely be objected...

Much has been said of late about...

Need I speak of...

Neither is it true that...

No objection can be brought against the...

No one will question...

Nobody really doubts that...

Not a few persons demand...

Nothing is more certain than...

Now it is evident...

Occasionally it is whispered that...

On the other hand, you will see...

One fact is clear...

Over and over again it has been shown that...

Some people think, indeed, that...

Some persons have expressed surprize that...

Strange as it may seem...

Strictly speaking, it is not...

Such is the truth...

That is quite obvious...

The contempt that is cast...

The fact is substantially true...

The fact, is that there is not...
The fact need not be concealed that...
The facts are before us all...
The language is perfectly plain...
The problem that presents itself is...
The time is not far distant when...
The time is short...
The truth of this has not been...
There are many people nowadays who...
There are people who tell you that...
There is no evidence that...
There is no mistaking the fact...
There is no other intelligible answer...
There is no parallel to...
There is no sufficient reason for...
There is none other...
There is not a shadow of...
There was a time when none denied it...
They did what they could...
This does not mean...
This is our last resort....
This is clearly perceived by...
This is especially true of...
This is very different from...
We all remember...
We are all aware that...
We are told that...
We know they will not...
We look around us...
We often speak of...
We will hear much in these days...
When I look around me...
You have the authority of

You tell me that...

PROPOSALS:

And it may be admitted that...
All experience evinces that...
Any thoughtful person can readily perceive...
But bear in mind that...
But I submit whether it...
But look at the difference...
But now, lastly, let us suppose...
But now let us turn to...
But you must remember...
Did time admit I could show you...
First, permit me to observe...
Here let me meet one other question...
I am sure you will allow me...
I am sure you will do me the justice...
I appeal to you on behalf of...
I ask your attention to this point...
I beg not to be interrupted here...
I certainly do not recommend...
I have been interested in hearing...
I have to appeal to you...
I hope you will acquit me of...
I invite you to consider...
I leave it to you to say...
I must now beg to ask...
I insist that you do not...
I think we should be willing to...
I want to invite your attention to...
I will call to mind this...

I wish to call your attention to...
I wish to know...
If I insist on this point here...
If we are conscious of...
If we find that...
In this situation, let us...
It is also to be borne in mind...
It is well that we clearly apprehend...
It remains for us to consider...
Let it be repeated...
Let it be for an instant supposed...
Let me add that...
Let me explain myself by saying...
Let me illustrate...
Let me instance in one thing only...
Let me put the subject before you...
Let me say one word further...
Let me tell you...
Let no one suppose that...
Let the truth be said outright...
Let these instances suffice...
Let us bear in mind that...
Let us consider that...
Let us go a step further....
Let us say frankly...
Let us see whether...
Let us stand together...
Let us look a little at...
Let us take, first of all...
Now for one moment let us...
Now let us observe what...
Now, on the other hand, let me...
Observe, if you please, that...

Permit me to add another circumstance...
Permit me to remind you...
Please remember that if...
To this end we must...
Truly...
We, in our turn, must...
We must not propose in...
We should pause to consider...
You may point, if you will, to...
You may search the history of...

CONFESSIONS:

I confess...
Certainly, I did not know...
For my part, I can say that I desire...
Here I have to speak of...
Here I wish I could stop
I admit it...
I admit, that if...
I am not ashamed to acknowledge...
I am speaking to-night for myself...
I am willing to admit that...
I confess I cannot help agreeing with...
I confess my notions are...
I confess that I like to dwell on...
I confess truly...
I dare say...
I dare say to you...
I do not pretend to believe...
I do not wish to be partial...
I do not wish you to suppose that...

I fear I only need refer to...
I grant, of course, that...
I grant that there are...
I grant, too, of course, that...
I have so high a respect for...
I have the confident hope that...
I know it is not uncommon for...
I know that this will sound strange...
I often wonder...
I personally doubt whether it...
I shall not suffer myself to...
I share the conviction of...
I should hold myself obliged to...
I speak in the most perfect honesty...
I trust it will not be considered ungenerous...
I trust we are not the type to...
I want to know whether...
I wish I could state...
I wish to say something about...
It is to my mind a...
It must be confessed that...
It was my good fortune...
Nevertheless, we must admit...
Perhaps, sir, I am mistaken in...
Readily we admit that...
The least desirable form of...
What we do say is...

QUESTIONS:

Am I mistaken in this?
And if it is further asked why...?

But is it in truth so easy to...?
But is it rationally conceivable that...?
But now, on the other hand, could...?
But the question for us is could it...?
But what is the motive?
But what then?
But why do we speak of...?
Can there be a better illustration than...?
Can you doubt it?
Does anybody believe that...?
Do you dream that...?
For what?
Has the person done...?
Have we any right to such a...?
How are we to explain this?
How do you account for...
I ask how you are going to...?
I ask myself...
I shall ask you one question...
I shall content myself with asking...
If I mistake not the sentiment of...
Is it fair to say that...?
Is it not evident that...?
Is it not quite possible that...?
Is it said that...?
Is not that the common sentiment?
Is there any reason for...?
It is a very serious question...
Let me ask who there is among us...
Now do you observe what follows from...
Now I want to ask whether...
Now perhaps you will ask me...
Now we come to the question...

Once more, how else could...?
The more I consider this question...
The question at issue is primarily...
The question is not...
The question presented is...
The question with me is...
This leads me to the question...
This is essentially a question of...
What are you asked to do?
What are you going to do?
What can be more intelligible than...?
What do you say to...?
What do we understand by...?
What has become of it?
What is the answer to all this?
What is this but an acknowledgment of
What is your opinion?
What then remains?
Who finds fault with these things?
Why should an argument be required to prove that...?
Why should it be necessary to confirm...?
Will you tell me how...?

NOTIFICATIONS:

And here, in passing, let us notice...
And here observe that...
And let me here again refer to...
But now some other things are to be noted...
For the sake of clearness...
I am advised that already...
I have been requested to say a word...

I pass by that...
I pass, then, from the question of...
I point you to...
I proceed to inquire into...
I quote from...
I shall attempt to show...
I shall presently show...
I shall sum up what has been said...
I shall, then, merely sum up...
I take leave to say...
I take the liberty of...
I turn now to another reason why...
I undertake to say...
I will allow more than this readily...
I will go no further...
I will not attempt to note the...
I will not enter into details...
I will not go into the evidence of...
I will not stop to inquire whether...
I will show you presently...
I will speak but a word or two more...
I wish to observe that...
If I hesitate, it is because...
If there is a person here...
I speak only for myself...
If you want to find out what...
It is necessary to account for...
It is not for me here to recall...
It is not my purpose to discuss...
It is not necessary that I define...
It is of importance that...
It is of very little importance what...
It is related of...

It is wholly unnecessary...
It is worthy of remark...
It may be a matter of doubt...
It may be shown that...
It may be suggested that...
It remains to...
It remains to be shown that...
Next, I observe that...
Now I have done...
Now, I proceed to examine...
Of the final issue I have no doubt...
One word more and I have done...
Our position is that...
Such an avowal is not...
Such is not my theory...
Such, then, is the answer where I make to...
Surely, I do not misinterpret the spirit...
The first point to be ascertained is...
The plea serves well with...
The point I wish to bring out...
The substance of all this is...
Then, I repeat...
There is a word which I wish to say...
There is another reason why...
There is one other point connected with...
There is one other point to which...
This brings me to a point on which...
This expectation was disappointed...
This I have already shown...
This relieves me of the necessity of...
To avoid all possibility of being...
To be sure...
To pass from that I notice...

To show all this is easy and certain...
To sum up, then...
We are all aware that...
We are here to discuss...
We are now able to determine...
We ought, first of all, to note...
We will not examine the proof of...
When it is recognized that...

IMPERATIVES:

Compare now the case of...
Do not entertain so weak an imagination...
Do not misunderstand me...
It must be recollected that...
Make no mistake...
You do not pretend that...

HYPOTHETICALS:

Did time admit I could show you...
I may be told that...
I may as well reply...
If anyone were to tell me...
If anyone is so short-sighted...
If I had my share...
If I must give an instance of this...
If I were asked what it is that...
If, perchance, one should say...
If such a thing were possible...
If such feelings were ever entertained...
If we accept at all the argument...

If we resign ourselves to facts...
In the last resort...
It may be supposed that...
That we might have done...
Unless I am wholly wrong...
Unless I greatly mistake the temper of...

EXAMPLES:

For instance...
If other evidence be wanting...
In answer to this singular theory...
In like manner...
In proof of this drift toward...
In something of a parallel...
In such cases...
In support of this claim...
In support of what I have been saying...
It reminds me of an anecdote...
Let me tell you a very interesting story...
Let us take an example in...
Now apply this to...
Only a few days ago...
Supposing, for instance...
Take, again, the case of...
Take the instance of...
To take a very different instance...
To show this in fact...
We have an instance in...

BREVITY

The most valuable of all talents is never using two words when one will do.

THOMAS JEFFERSON

Last tip: be brief.

NEED A COACHING SESSION?

The mind is not a vessel to be filled, but a fire to be kindled.

Thank you for reaching the end of this book and leaving a kind review!

When I started this project, I had intended to write almost five-hundred pages surmising the near-entirety of my teachings and findings. However, my editor kindly suggested that such a voluminous work may frighten the more timid reader. I therefore intend to write several more books on similar topics which I hope will add value to those interested in growing their communication skills.

Many hours of writing, research and sometimes frustration have gone into its production. Yet, I hope it has given you just a glimpse of what I provide my clients in their one-to-one coaching sessions.

If you would like a bespoke coaching session to help improve your thinking, communication skills or voice, as thanks for purchasing this book, I would like to offer you a 20% discount. No matter what your needs, I would be happy to help you to become a better communicator!

You can contact me on LinkedIn or at

Booking@RichardDiBritannia.com

NOTES

Pictographs, Profanities and Poor Vocabularies:

1. DeFrank, M. and Kahlbaugh, P. (2018). *Language Choice Matters: When Profanity Affects How People Are Judged.* Journal of Language and Social Psychology. Vol 38, Issue 1.
2. Frost, S. A. (1869). *Frost's Laws and By-Laws of American Society. A Condensed but Thorough Treatise on Etiquette and Its Usages in America Containing Plain and Reliable Directions for Deportment in Every Situation in* Life. Dick & Fitzgerald, America.
3. Washington, G. (1776). *General Orders, 3 August 1776.* Head Quarters, New York.

Dispelling Genius:

1. Marden, O. S. (1911). *Pushing to the Front.* The Success Company. New York.

How is Eloquent Speaking Different from a Golden Voice:

1. Hedin, Benjamin, ed. (2004). Studio A: The Bob Dylan Reader. W.W. Norton & Co
2. Julio, R. et al. (2014) *Breaking the News: First Impressions Matter on Online News.* Federal University of Minas Gerais, Brazil. Available at: https://arxiv.org/pdf/1503.07921v2.pdf

How You Think Impacts How You Speak:

1. Gadkari, P. (2013) *Laser Listening: Could you Eavesdrop on the Guardian?* BBC News. Available at: https://www.bbc.co.uk/news/technology-23793465

Struggling to Articulate Your Thoughts May be by Design:

1. Holmes, E. (1911). *What Is and What Might Be.* Page 128. Constable and Co Ltd.
2. Stephens, W. B. (1998). *Education in Britain 1750-1914.* Macmillan.
3. Graham, F. P. (1972). *Court Exempts the Amish From Going to High School – May 16, 1972.* The New York Times.
4. Chitty, C. (2007). *Eugenics, Race and Intelligence in Education.* Continuum.

Rhetoric – It's not Just Rhyme, Rhythm and Reason:

1. Binkley, R. (2004), *The Rhetoric of Origins and the Other: Reading the Ancient Figure of Enheduanna*. State University of New York Press. Pages 47–64.
2. Hutto, D. (2002), *Ancient Egyptian Rhetoric in the Old and Middle Kingdoms*, Rhetorica, 20 (3), Pages 213–33.
3. Forsyth, W. (1849). *Hortensius: Or, The Advocate: An Historical Essay*. London.
4. Lipson, C. and Binkley, R. (2004) *Rhetoric Before and Beyond the Greeks*. Albany, NY: State U of New York Press. Page 122.
5. Roos, D. (2019) *Seven Ways the Printing Press Changed the World*. History.com. Available at: https://www.history.com/news/printing-press-renaissance
6. C. N. Douglas, (1917). *Forty Thousand Quotations: Prose and Poetical*. Halcyon House. United States of America.

The Power of Metaphors:

1. Musolff, A. (2010) *Metaphor, Nation and the Holocaust*. Routledge.
2. Musolff, A. [n.d]. *Dehumanizing metaphors in UK immigrant debates in press and online media*. University of East Anglia. Available at: https://core.ac.uk/download/pdf/192559377.pdf
3. Pilyarchuck, K. Onysko, A. (2018) *Conceptual Metaphors in Donald Trump's Political Speeches: Framing his Topics and (Self-)Constructing his*

Persona. New Collegium Philologies. Available at:
https://www.researchgate.net/publication/
330528204_Conceptual_Metaphors_in_Don-
ald_Trump's_ Political_Speeches_Framing_his_-
Topics_and_Self-Constructing_his_Persona

4. Clarkson, J. [n.d] *Top Gear.* BBC.
5. Wiggins, N. (2012) *Stop using military metaphors for disease.* British Medical Journal. Available at:
https://www.bmj.com/content/345/bmj.e4706

How Public Speaking Could Bring You Wealth:

1. Vine, J. (2019). *My Boris Johnson Story. The Spectator.*
Available at: https://www.spectator.co.uk/article/my-
boris-johnson-story
2. Yoon, R. (2016). *$153 million in Bill and Hillary Clinton speaking fees, documented.* CCN. Available
at: https://edition.cnn.com/2016/02/05/poli-
tics/hillary-clinton-bill-clinton-paid-
speeches/index.html

ABOUT THE AUTHOR

Richard Di Britannia is an expert voice, speech and communication skills coach. His unique 'thought-articulation' method is used by senior executives at Google, Amazon and Microsoft.

For over a decade Richard has also worked as a voice actor and video narrator for top global brands, institutions and organisations, all beginning when he was rendered mute by acid reflux and had to teach himself how to talk again.

He has also published an international best-seller on the topic of improving enunciation, building vocal strength and linguistic fluency with 'Speak and Be Heard: 101 Vocal Exercises for Voice Actors, Public Speakers and Professionals'.

You can contact Richard for a coaching session at

Booking@RichardDiBritannia.com

Made in the USA
Middletown, DE
23 September 2023